The Art of the
Documentary

Ten Conversations with Leading Directors,
Cinematographers, Editors, and Producers

Meg

D1387093

· 000244554 ·

The Art of the Documentary
Ten Conversations with Leading Directors, Cinematographers, Editors, and Producers

Megan Cunningham

New Riders
1249 Eighth Street
Berkeley, CA 94710
510/524-2178
800/283-9444
510/524-2221 (fax)

Find us on the Web at www.peachpit.com.
To report errors, please send a note to errata@peachpit.com
New Riders is an imprint of Peachpit, a division of Pearson Education.

Editor: Douglas Cruickshank
Senior Executive Editor: Marjorie Baer
Production Editor: Hilal Sala
Copy Editor: Doug Adrianson
Compositor: Kim Scott
Photo Editor: Annie Young Frisbie
Indexer: Julie Bess
Cover design: Mimi Heft
Interior design: Mimi Heft with Kim Scott

Notice of Rights

Notice of Liability

Trademarks

ISBN 0-321-31623-1

9 8 7 6 5 4 3 2 1

Printed and bound in the United States of America

This book is dedicated to Larry Silk, A.C.E., a generous mentor to so many, who taught me a deep respect for the craft, to enjoy the rewards of creative work, and to maintain integrity above all else.

Table of Contents

Acknowledgments

This book project, like the films it discusses, was a true collaboration.

Each person who consented to be interviewed for *The Art of the Documentary* far exceeded the conventional expectations of such involvement. All were extraordinarily generous in donating time and insights to help me create this book, and it was remarkable to witness their connection to the subject—digging through boxes in attics to uncover rare photos, pursuing long-forgotten factual information, and allowing me to conduct follow-up conversations. Their support of my project was a great compliment to me, and their devotion to documentary filmmaking is a gift to readers.

At Peachpit/New Riders, I'd like to thank senior executive editor Marjorie Baer, who enthusiastically participated in my early brainstorming and championed this book throughout. She is rare person: a caring listener and an acquisitions editor willing to take a risk for a project she believes in. Without her creativity, guidance, and support, it is unlikely that we would have embarked on the current book beyond the original concept. I'd also like to thank product marketing manager Damon Hampson and publicist Sara Jane Todd, who handle a remarkable number of book marketing initiatives with grace and a personal touch. Copy editor Doug Adrianson deserves a medal for his fast, meticulous work. Designer Mimi Heft, production editor Hilal Sala, compositor Kim Scott, and manufacturing manager Jenny Collins are the invisible hands who made the book you're holding so beautiful.

Here in New York, I was assisted by another remarkable group. My creative research and licensing team—Wendy Cohen, Jessica Buritica, and Stacey Sperling—provided the necessary foundation on which the entire book is built. Throughout the six-month interview process, my transcriber Jamie Pastor Bolnick—an accomplished author in her own right—was on call virtually all hours of the day and night.

I've received daily encouragement from my own production company, Magnet Media. Dave Marcus, Dylan Lorenz, Jessica Buritica, Colin Yu, William Johnson, Bill Ehrlich, Lisa Snyder, Monique Nijhout, Heidi Muhleman, Dan Lafferty, and Dalmar James all inspired me throughout the long hours of this project, and they continue to make every working day more gratifying.

There are a of number people in the film, television, and media industry who may not see their contributions directly reflected in this text, but who have provided me with the confidence to take on a project of this scale and ambition. I'd like to thank just a few: Alex Juhasz, Trina Quagliaroli, Barbara Kopple, Richard Pena, Kirk Paulsen, Brian Schmidt, Jonathan Franzen, Lynn True, Ellen Kuras, Reid Rosefelt, Sharon Sklar, Edet Belzberg, Haskell Wexler, Carol Dysinger, Terry Ragan, Dion Scopettulo, Garrett Rice, Ferida Nydam, Paul Saccone, Brian Meaney, Greg Niles, Michael Pinkman, Eric Thomas, Michael Wong, Bill Hudson, Susan Marshall, Patty Montesion, Michael Horton, Cheryl Adler, Kristan Jiles, Mark Cokes, Steve Kilisky, Steve Bayes, Daniel Brown, Ted Schilowitz, Dave Tecson, Terry Lawler, Linda Kahn, Michelle Materre, Marcie Setlow, Alan Oxman, Jean Tsien, Patty White, Scott Greenberg, Pola Rappaport, Julian Hobbs, Chris Trent, Christine Mitsogiorgakis, Evan Schechtman, Matthew Cohen, Inger Lund, Bill Werde, Heather Moore, Kim Reid, Kira Pollack, the Debevoises, Doug Sayles, Stephanie Kwok, Kenrick Cato, and Dominic Milano.

My photo editor and assistant, Annie Frisbie, put tireless effort and creative participation into this project. I only wish I'd known to bring her on board sooner. Her contributions are visible on every page, from securing permissions for every image, to checking every fact and every caption. Annie is also a gifted filmmaker, writer, and teacher.

The true hero of this project is my immensely talented editor, Douglas Cruickshank. From his first day on the book until the last, he lent me personal advice and expert guidance, sharing seasoned professional practices. Beyond the scope of traditional editing, he helped hone my interview process, shared his intimate familiarity with the film industry, and with his uncommon wit and dependable instincts, made even the daunting parts of the production enjoyable. My gratitude to him is beyond words.

Finally, every time I undertake a new project, my parents, friends, and family inevitably see more potential than I can imagine fulfilling. I rely on this network more than any other, and I am grateful for their faith. It means everything to me.

Foreword

BY BARBARA KOPPLE

For me, documentary filmmaking has always been about taking the time to go beneath the surface and find the heart of the story. Documentary filmmakers create unforgettable and entertaining films that introduce us to people we never would have known, or show us a different side of people we thought we knew already. Great nonfiction filmmakers take us halfway around the world, or maybe just to the other side of the tracks, but either way, it's a journey that can change us forever. What makes this journey possible is collaboration with other directors, with camera people and editors, and with the subjects of their films.

I learned in the beginning of my filmmaking career that collaboration was part of successful and powerful documentaries. My first job in the industry was working for Albert and David Maysles, who strove to create a family-like atmosphere while working. We screened footage together and listened to each other's opinions. It gave me a sense that what I said mattered. The Maysles were doing more than creating documentary films; they were creating a community of documentary filmmakers.

This idea of community came into play on the film *Winter Soldier,* which captured the testimony of veterans after they returned from the Vietnam War. This film was made by a collective of 15 independent filmmakers in collaboration with the Vietnam Veterans Against the War. During the many months of editing, the filmmakers and some Vietnam veterans lived and worked together in a house in Allamuchy, New Jersey. While cooking together and taking turns doing different chores, we screened material and discussed it as a group. This intense, collaborative living and working situation created an environment where everyone could contribute their diverse opinions and ideas to the film.

Perhaps the greatest collaboration in documentary film is between the filmmaker and the subject. Documentary filmmakers encourage and inspire subjects to tell their story, and subjects learn to trust the filmmaker to tell it with honesty and integrity. During the shooting of *Harlan County, USA*, we lived with the striking miners and their families and formed an intense bond with them. Even when we couldn't afford to buy film stock, we stood on the picket line alongside the miners. It was an honor to have become a close part of their lives and to tell their story.

I have been fortunate to have collaborated with several of the filmmakers included in this book: Sheila Nevins, the fearless president of HBO Documentary where she has given so many filmmakers an opportunity to show their work; Kirsten Johnson, the talented cinematographer, whom I worked with on the films *My Generation, American Standoff,* and *The Hamptons,* and who is now shooting and directing her own films; the brilliant Larry Silk, who edited so many of my films— *American Dream, Wild Man Blues, Fallen Champ: The Untold Story of Mike Tyson,* and *The Hamptons*—is a true storyteller.

Every talented person included in this book, and many more, are part of a larger documentary community where we respect each other and support each other's work. I am privileged to work in this industry and to be in the company of such wonderful and creative people. In Megan Cunningham's book, documentary filmmakers and filmgoers alike will get the rare opportunity to meet some of these amazing documentarians who reveal so much about their art.

Are Documentaries Art?

When I first sat down to interview Chris Hegedus and D A Pennebaker, they asked me the title of this book. My answer kicked off a lively discussion on the validity of classifying documentaries as art.

● ● ●

DAP: I think that documentaries—films in general—are different in most people's minds from what they consider art. They know that paintings, which cost $16 to paint and now sell for $120 million, have to be an art form, because nothing else could account for that value. But I think that the films are not really art. Perhaps old films, and European films are sometimes—because of the way they're dealt with. But you would hardly consider 90 percent of the films that get released to be an art form if you were seriously thinking about art. And I think the documentary has somehow found its way under the shadow of the film.

MC: You don't consider any film or video to be art?

DAP: I think there *are* films—and I remember them—which were considered art forms. They were unconventional films, done by various performers. Films like *Meshes in the Afternoon*—all of Maya Deren's films. Those were definitely art films because they couldn't show in any other circumstance. You'd never release them in theaters.

MC: Experimental films you'd classify as art, but not documentaries?

DAP: Right. There were a whole bunch of films that appeared then that were absolutely considered art films, but nobody ever saw them. And that was partly why they were considered art films. Because nobody had to look at them! But films that you looked at, you generally thought of as entertainment and not art.

CH: Megan, you're not really saying that the documentary *is* art, but more that there's an art to making documentaries? Is that what you're talking about?

MC: It's both. The book is an appreciation of documentary work, as an art form. And at the same time it will be read by people in the film and television industry who are looking for a way to replace the "missing mentor," the phenomenon of the apprentice/mentor relationship disappearing in the digital age. I guess that's my own bias. I know so many people whose first film was a total disaster because they didn't have anyone who could teach them the craft of filmmaking. They understand how to use professional equipment, and can afford to buy or to rent it now with the changing economics of digital production, but they have no understanding of the techniques used by accomplished filmmakers. It's no longer an elite group of people making film and television today, which is exciting from a democratic perspective. But it's disappointing from a quality standpoint, because there's no "passing on" the art of visual storytelling.

DAP: In the world of art, as we grew up learning it, somebody held up a Van Gogh and said, "Here is a work of art." And then you go to the museum and you see a lot of things that aren't anywhere up to Van Gogh's level of quality, but you still call them works of art. And they may be totally failed and thrown out on the street, but they're still works of art. The films that we've seen in the last couple days—we're supposed to be looking at films for the Academy [of Motion Picture Arts and Sciences Awards, the Oscars]—the long-form documentaries I would not call art. And that doesn't mean that I don't think they're good films, but I would not call any of them works of art. Would you?

CH: I definitely would. I think they're all individual statements. Each one is very different in terms of the style, and each is coming from a director's point of view. The way that we make our films is very much like an artist, because we tend to take on a lot of the roles ourselves. We are actually the people who *film* the film, and *edit* the film, and whatever directing there is in a real-life film, I suppose you could say we're doing that too. Which, really, for me always harks back to my background in the

> *"It's no longer an elite group of people making film and television, which is exciting from a democratic perspective."*

arts, where you don't have somebody else, usually, paint the painting for you, or making your canvas. So my step into making films was very much in that same spirit.

DAP: All the films we make, in your head you classify them as a form of art? I'd like to, but I guess I don't.

CH: I do. I mean, even though some are more commercially based.

DAP: No, you're grading them. And I don't think you *grade* art. That's the thing; it fails or it doesn't fail, but you don't say, "This is better than that," unless you're judging a show or something, and then you have to. To say that Vermeer is better than Van Gogh is ridiculous. I have the same problem in films. Saying one film is somehow better than another is a waste of time.

CH: You're asking me if I think of film as being an art form or not. And I feel like it is, or can be. It's also a very commercial medium, in a way that most painting doesn't get to be because it's not so economically involved. I think that's where everything blurs.

> *"You're not really saying that the documentary is art, but more that there's an art to making documentaries?"*

DAP: There's this incredible rift that occurred around the beginning of the 20th century. It was in the '20s when suddenly there were a number of really good publishers able to publish large quantities of books. Everyone became a Hemingway and a Fitzgerald. There were hundreds of them. A lot of them have fallen away now, but that was a period when a whole lot of incredible writing talent emerged, and different from what had been before, from the few writers in the 19th century.

And it's happened again recently, partly because of 9/11, because it was like the Zapruder footage [of the John F. Kennedy assassination]—what we saw was *accidental*. People just happened to film it, and it created a whole new sense of what documentary should be: an accidental interception, somehow, of the real world with somebody who happens to be there—which goes against the kind of primitive concept of storytelling, the Byronic sense of the artist that we all carry around, nurtured in the fourth grade somewhere, cutting little pieces of paper out, pinning them on the windows. So I think you're going to have that now with film and particularly with documentary. People just assume anybody can do it, because it has that quality. But they're not going to go and buy a $500 camera and go out and expect to make a lot of money with it. They don't know what to do.

MC: You're saying that our concept of what documentary is has changed since 9/11. It's now drama caught on film haphazardly rather than purposeful storytelling?

DAP: Everyone can feel that we've worn out the possibilities of something else, and so we needed to find something new to stuff in the stocking.

MC: Audiences have grown tired of the expected narrative films, and want something fresh.

DAP: I think that's what's coming up. Because now it's perceived that there is money in the distribution of documentary. It was before Michael Moore, too. And I think what always happens is, the minute you've indicated that there's money available, people with talent are drawn to it like flies. It isn't just that they want the money, but the money guarantees that there'll be some distribution.

MC: What does that mean for first-time documentary filmmakers?

DAP: They have to find their way into this peculiar world, which is now inhabited by a whole lot of different individuals, and as I'm sure you've found, as different as you could get. If you went out and did this for painting, I'm sure most of the painters probably go to the same bar, go to the same place in Maine. They have a lot of similarities. And I don't think you find that in the people making documentary films. I mean Chris was an art student, in effect, doing photography, and making photographic imagery which, for her, constituted art, because she wanted to think of herself as an artist, so she had to create art. I got involved in documentary because somebody showed me a film, and I said, "Shit, I could do that." And the guy that showed it to me I knew was an artist. But I didn't think of it as having made me become an artist. I'm not sure Ken Burns does. I don't think Barbara Kopple does. I don't know whether Al Maysles does—Al really thinks of himself as a kind of therapist, on the other end of a camera, which somehow induces therapy into people's lives.

"The book is part appreciation and part celebration of the craft of documentary making."

MC: I am not trying to find the commonalities. Actually, I hope that there's a lot of conflict within the book—and so far there is—in the same way that smart policy makers can disagree on an approach to the same social problem. The book is part appreciation and part exploration of the craft of documentary making. It's also a discussion of various approaches to the work, by different crew members. I'm not trying to distill the essence of how you make a documentary artful.

DAP: But we all have to make the same thing, because it has to fit into the same box. That's the problem. If we want to make any money on it, it's got to be 90 minutes long, or one hour, or whatever it is. And it has to have a beginning and closing titles, and it has to have certain things in it. Normally, it's decorating. None of us would get into that if we had a choice.

Directing

Respectfully Collaborating

In the world of mainstream features, film directors select and harness the crew, live through endless revisions of the script, foster ingratiating relationships with pricey talent, scout and scrutinize locations, and oversee the design of extravagant costumes, makeup, and sets—all to create the illusion of a cinematic reality. Documentary directors arrive on the "scene" of their participants' everyday life (with or without their micro-crew) with far less fanfare. For most, the less conspicuous they are, the better. Because of the importance of the personal relationship between documentary directors and their subjects, the director may appear indistinguishable from the film subject's family or friends during a shoot.

The role of a documentary director varies considerably from project to project, and from filmmaker to filmmaker. Great documentaries have had origins in the dark depths of a research center; others have been born out of curiosity in street graffiti, and still others out of decades-old home movie video-diaries. There is very little that is similar in how two directors approach the same topic, or even how they'd define legitimate, film-worthy subject matter.

Despite varied approaches, the relationship a director forms with a film's subject is critical. As cinema verité director Chris Hegedus describes it, "I think you can't help but want to protect your characters in the film, especially in situations where you become friends with them, which we were in *Startup.com*. There were so many different aspects during the process of making that film that were difficult for me as a filmmaker. One was that in filming the dissolving of a relationship I was party to certain information that I felt like I wanted to pass on to the other person, and tell them. But I couldn't quite do it, because even as filmmakers we didn't really know the whole story. So you just have to let what happens, happen. In *front* of you! And then when you're editing it, you also want to be protective of them. You don't want to make somebody seem like they're jerky, or being villainous, or being a victim, because everybody in their lives is all of those things at one point. There's a time that you're a victim, there's a time that you're a villain. As a filmmaker, it's very complicated. The hardest thing is when you show the film to the people in it, and they see themselves."

Director Errol Morris—whose work in many ways stands as a critique of cinema verité filmmaking—sees himself as an investigator exploring subjectivity, exploring "How people see the world, their mental landscape, their own private way of seeing themselves and the world around them." Rather than follow his subjects throughout their day, capturing their mundane activities and waiting for a moment of natural drama, Morris brings his characters into a studio where he controls the scope of the conversation. Peering at them directly with his image projected in front of them through the Interrotron, a dual TelePrompTer contraption he invented, Morris uses an assertive interview style to encourage his participants to tell their story in what he calls "true first person" cinema.

His stylized editing reveals exceptional aspects of the subject's story, but his documentaries are heavily directed. Morris's films possess a controlled editorial voice, draped in dramatic musical scores and lavish cinematography. Through fictional reenactments, moviegoers are given Morris's interpretation of what the interviewee's stories might look like. Of his extensive interviews in *The Fog of War* with Robert McNamara—whom he met the first day of the shoot—Morris says, "It was not even clear that he would ever come back or if he came back, as he did many times, whether he would continue to cooperate with the film, whether he was *interested* in the film. I'm amazed he actually went through it, and I'm even more amazed that we're still on speaking terms."

"A predictable topic when documentary makers get together over a beer is always what is or is not documentary. Allegiance to fact is fundamental, but Grierson's 'the creative treatment of actuality' is pretty good, and Zola's 'A work of art is a corner of nature seen through a temperament' is even better. There are no rules in this young art form, only decisions about where to draw lines and how to remain consistent to the contract you will set up with your audience."

—*Michael Rabiger,* Directing the Documentary

While *The Fog of War* is devoted to McNamara's story, Morris also uses the Vietnam-era Secretary of Defense's biography to explore larger ideas. "If you were trying to make a movie about the 20th century in some oddball fashion, but still nevertheless trying to grab ahold of the 20th century, you could do no better than to create a profile of this man. History can easily become overburdened by details. And so, in telling history, you have to chart a course through a morass of material. You have to tell a story, and you have to communicate the story powerfully."

To chart that course, documentary directors rely on a core team of collaborators, people who contribute more than a 9-to-5 crew. In the documentary filmmaking community, leading directors frequently work with the same group of top cinematographers, researchers, producers, and editors. Still, collaboration can be immensely difficult. As veteran editor Geof Bartz says, "There's that saying that 70 percent of any project is figuring out how to get along with the people you're working with. I don't know how you can work in this business without embracing the collaboration."

For Morris, one of his strongest alliances on *The Fog of War* was with McNamara, his film subject. "I saw the movie as a collaboration. Not that I allowed him to completely push me around, but that somehow I was trying not to create a brief against him for some imagined war crimes tribunal. I was trying to uncover how he saw the world, the complexities of his personality. I was trying to understand him."

Ken Burns's production company, Florentine Films, is made up of a close-knit group. "We have less of a civilized circumstance, the model of a corporation, and more of a heroic one—that is to say, we're grabbing from the filmmaking family that we've worked with for years." On the group's ambitious multiyear films, teamwork is key. With Burns and with other directors, much of their strongest work was created by welcoming, and acknowledging, contributions from an array of team members and others. However, there is never a lack of clarity as to who is in command. Burns says, "The thing is, it *is* autocratic: Somebody has to be responsible for making the decision at the end of the day, and that person is me. But until that moment that you have to do it, it's a better process to be open to anybody. So, you can come in and sit in the editing room, and your opinion is as valued as anybody's. We love that sense of participation."

Collaborators D A Pennebaker and Chris Hegedus, who happen to be married, have worked together on dozens of films. Hegedus says their collaboration works "because we have similar views. And in the same way that access to your characters and story has to do a lot with respect for the people that you're filming, and what they're doing in their lives, and the privilege of being let into their lives, what makes a good collaboration between filmmakers is respect for their work and their abilities. Having respect for the films Pennebaker did before we became partners allowed me to have a wonderful collaboration with him. Because his input is always very important to me. Even when we disagree. During every film, we usually do get divorced once!"

As Michael Rabiger wisely recommends in his guidebook for new directors, "Take time to understand your crew's concerns and problems, and make every effort to include them in conceptual considerations of the film. This, in turn, invites suggestions that may not be practical or desirable. Unless everyone understands from the outset that only a director can decide ultimately what goes into a film, the director's openness may be misconstrued as an invitation to make the film by committee."

The openness and criticism required in respectful collaboration must be handled diplomatically, as in the end a director's actions in part define both the filmmaker and the film. For some directors, it's vital to interact with a film's subjects socially, for the sake of the film. As D A Pennebaker says, "That's the way the film gets made, in that joining together, hanging out with the people, so that they don't deal with you as a photographic process. They deal with you as somebody who knows them and can respond to something they're going to tell you, some piece of the news. And the camera is totally invisible—they don't see it anymore. It disappears. And that's *really* interesting. Because for me it has a primitive aspect. This kind of filming goes back to the way people behaved long, long ag; thousands of years ago, when they dealt with conversation and the languages, two families who lived as tribes would meet, they could hardly talk to each other because they didn't share the same language. They certainly didn't share the ability to write, but they had to find ways of transmitting information and ideas. It came by concentrating, they had to *look* very hard, they had to try to understand body language, and all sorts of things that we've thrown away now. That aspect, that driving need to *find out* things, propels this filmmaking when it's good, when it works."

Ken Burns

Director

Inhabiting History

"**M**ORE AMERICANS GET THEIR HISTORY FROM KEN BURNS THAN any other source," historian Stephen Ambrose said. Indeed, Burns's films are perhaps the most recognizable, and among the most widely seen contemporary American documentaries.

Burns specializes in taking well-researched, comprehensive historical narrative out of academia and bringing it to life as artful, dramatic storytelling. The status and familiarity his work has obtained is due in part to the sheer length of his historical series, but it's also because he has always produced them for the Public Broadcasting Service's potential audience of 100 million viewers. By selecting human-interest topics—baseball, the Civil War, and jazz—and conveying their evolution through well-told anecdotes, photographs, and music, Burns reaches people who are unaccustomed to watching historical documentaries. In fact, his spacious series, done in his signature style featuring lush archival photographs and slow, melodic voiceovers, have all but dominated public television for the past 30 years.

Ken Burns filmography

In 1976, after graduating from Hampshire College in Amherst, Massachusetts, Burns founded Florentine Films in his New York apartment with Buddy Squires, Roger Sherman, and Larry Hott. Burns led the way in bringing archival material to life by using narration from diverse sources: juxtaposing everyday citizens's diaries and letters with traditional interviews of historical experts. Together with editor and coproducer Paul Barnes, Burns combines these carefully recorded voiceovers, interviews, and sound effects to dramatize historical events in rich, emotionally charged fashion. This oral history technique of incorporating a chorus of voices with diverse relationships to the topic at hand displays a rich tapestry of American history that deepens viewers's appreciation of the subject, be it a time period, a president, a sport, a war, or a statue.

"If I have any skill in the editing room," Burns says, "it's to be just a regular person looking at this thing going, wait a second, I don't understand that, why are they assuming this? And that's how I fix the films in the editing." Through Burns's eyes, America, one of the world's youngest countries, is shown its own dramatic, complex history, mined from visual and audio archives, revealed through beautiful cinematography and the voices of everyday people.

Burns's research process—famous within the film world—is driven by his knack for uncovering intriguing correspondence, diminutive but revealing historical details, and uncommon artifacts. These particulars are carefully crafted into large-scale television series, but they give his films a visual texture, depth, and emotional authenticity that more closely resembles an independent film than the traditional documentary born out of news journalism. Burns's dedication to research is inspired, in part, by an awareness of the accountability he has in popularizing history. "The subjects of these films have been an opportunity to practice and improve my craft of filmmaking. That in their totality they represent a fairly diverse and complicated view of American history is secondary, but not insignificant. I know that. And I know that people get a lot of their history from me. So there's a responsibility for me, always, to do the very best I can each time out. Everybody with a video camera is going to look to people who know how to tell stories as a mentor."

He is best known for his trilogy of epic documentary series: *The Civil War*, *Jazz*, and *Baseball*. However, dozens of Burns's historical films have played at film festivals and aired on PBS, including *Brooklyn Bridge*; *Lewis and Clark: The Journey of the Corps of Discovery*; *Frank Lloyd Wright*; *Mark Twain*; *Thomas Jefferson*; *Unforgivable Blackness: The Rise and Fall of Jack Johnson*; *Empire of the Air: The Men Who Made Radio*; *The West,* and numerous others.

Burns has earned his home on PBS through persistent fund-raising from private and public foundations. And though his projects focus on topics with broad appeal, Burns's approach often results in revitalizing interest in individuals, such as boxer Jack Johnson, or phenomena, such as the development of radio, that long ago drifted from the center of popular culture. Race relations, for example, are explored throughout most of his films—not in a dry, academic way, but in a manner that exposes the impact prejudice has had on real people's lives, and how that impact has affected the course of history.

Well before his programs are broadcast, Burns "sings" about his work through an active public relations and marketing campaign that is not unlike those employed for major Hollywood film releases. "Evangelism is a very important and often neglected part of making documentaries," he says. "With so many channels you can make a great film that nobody sees. So you have to go out and sing about it."

Director Ken Burns. Through Burns's eyes, America, one of the world's youngest countries, is shown its own dramatic, complex history, mined from visual and audio archives, and revealed through beautiful cinematography and the voices of everyday people.

Photo courtesy of Florentine Films.

●　●　●

When did you first develop an interest in film?

I have to go back a pretty long way to think of a time when I didn't want to be a filmmaker. I suppose I went through the fireman and the astronaut stages as a little boy, but almost from the beginning of my life I wanted to be a filmmaker.

What attracted you to film at such an early age?

My father had an extremely strict curfew after my mother died, and yet he forgave it generously. If there was a film playing at the local cinema in Ann Arbor, Michigan, where I grew up, or if there was something on television that might last, on a school night, until 2 a.m., I could stay up. The first time I ever saw my father cry was when he was watching a film. So I knew there was some power in this medium, and I was absolutely convinced by the time I was done with high school—having digested thousands of films, written many capsule reviews of thousands of films I had seen, and devoured film books—that I wanted to be the next Howard Hawkes or Alfred Hitchcock or, most of all, John Ford, who is my idol.

When did your interest change from Hollywood movies to documentary filmmaking?

I ended up at Hampshire College, where all the film and photography teachers were mostly social documentary still photographers. They disabused me of this interest in the Hollywood film, and reminded me of what power there is in the things that are and were. True things.

Did you receive formal training in filmmaking?

None of this stuff is teachable in a real way. You can have great teachers who are, by their example, helpful. And I had two tremendous mentors—Jerome Liebling at Hampshire College and Elaine Mays, also a still photographer, at Hampshire College. And the stuff they imparted didn't happen in the classroom. It wasn't didactic. It was something else. And I really treasure what they gave me.

Film wasn't an afterthought, but it wasn't their primary thing. My teachers were social documentary still photographers, and they combined this with a heavy respect for the power of the individual to convey complex information. I found myself totally turned around, disinterested in Hollywood feature films. But I was still passionate about narrative, combined with a completely untrained and untutored interest in American history, which I'd always had.

Ken Burns and Roger Sherman during the shooting of *Brooklyn Bridge.* **Burns and Sherman were classmates at Hampshire College, In 1976 they cofounded Florentine Films with Buddy Squires and Larry Hott.**

Photo courtesy of Florentine Films.

Did you know right away that you would be making historical films?

I had not taken any courses in American history since 11th grade, when they hold a gun to your head and tell you that you have to take it. And I found, in one of these incredibly fortuitous moments, not only what I wanted to do but who I was; I consider it really lucky. There was some moment at the end of my experience at Hampshire College, when I did not recognize the person who went in and the person who went out. I was already working on a history project that had gotten under my skin, and I was making a film in school for Old Sturbridge Village, which was the Colonial Williamsburg of New England. And I suddenly realized every cell in my body was firing, and it was great. I knew I was going to make documentaries, and I knew I would make historical documentaries.

Why did you gravitate toward history as your subject matter?

I've chosen history, but I'm not interested in history per se. It's what I work in. It's where I practice my craft. The word *history* is mostly made up of the word *story*. I'm interested in telling stories.

Style and Storytelling

Over the past two decades, you and your collaborators at Florentine Films have developed a style of making history films that has dominated PBS nonfiction programming and has been imitated by many filmmakers. It's become so recognizable, Apple Computer even named an effect after you—the Ken Burns effect—which allows users of its iMovie software to pan-and-scan a photograph. Many call it the Ken Burns brand of filmmaking. Do you feel you've created a genre?

The PBS people talk to me about brand all the time, and I just shiver as if I've walked past a graveyard. But I understand what you mean.

When you mention the words "Ken Burns film," it's really important to know that I'm the cipher who stands in for a great number of very talented people who also make up this style: writers like Dayton Duncan and Geoffrey Ward, cinematographers like Buddy Squires and Alan Moore, editors like Paul Barnes, Patricia Reidy, and Eric Ewres, and coproducers like Lynn Novick, Dayton Duncan, and Paul Barnes. It's a family.

Getting back to your question about genre, any production is a series of literally a million problems or more. And I don't say "problems" in a negative sense. Each time you set out to create something you're faced with resistance and obstacles—and that's a problem. And you have to decide each time how you're going to handle these million, million problems. In this particular area, how you generally respond to the larger, theoretical problems can vaguely be called style. The technique that you employ to solve problems, if it's organic and true to you, becomes your style. It's not a fixed thing, it's always evolving.

Do you disagree with the critics who say you have a recurring style?

It is true that if my films were like photographs in a gallery, you could line them up on a wall and say they look more or less the same, but each individual film is so uniquely different from the others that style, in the end, just becomes a description of how one solves the problems of production.

The Florentine Films family. Ken Burns and longtime coproducer Dayton Duncan with the *Mark Twain* production crew, in 1991. Burns says, "We have less of a civilized circumstance, the model of a corporation, and more of a heroic one—that is to say, we're grabbing from the filmmaking family that we've worked with for years."

Photo by Robert Sargent Fay. Courtesy of Florentine Films.

We also see that people adopt technique *without* it being organic, in the sense that it doesn't originate from the material they're working with. People say, "Oh, people are copying your style all the time on the History Channel." But I say, "It's doesn't matter." There's no copyright on how you solve a problem. It's just whether it's authentic to your process, and to you as an artist or a craftsperson, and whether it works.

> *"We've never abandoned a project because there wasn't enough stuff."*

In a way, style becomes the stepping-stone for larger artistic, psychological, spiritual, historical, and metaphorical issues that any production inevitably brings up—whether it's a film, a photograph, a painting, theater, whatever it is. I understand that there are wonderful parodies that make fun of my quote unquote "style." Jay Leno spoofed it, and David Letterman spoofed it. It's great.

For me, it's employed only in the service of trying to authentically work out the problems of the project I'm working on at that moment. And if you have to jettison a traditional approach to prove that it is an aspect of your style, because the particular project demands it in a moment, so be it. If, in the face of criticism that this is the way you always do it, too bad. I'm not hoping to satisfy a critic's view of what I should be doing but, in fact, trying to work it out. I mean, Cézanne painted the same mountain over and over and over and over again, trying to work out something. It's very, very personal—*very* personal. I think that style is the stepping-stone to the larger questions about being, and art, and storytelling.

Your aesthetic approach relies heavily on archival photographs, documents, and paintings. What happens when you tackle a project where there is not a large archive of images to draw from?

Well, we've never abandoned a project because there wasn't enough stuff. We just sort of try to figure out how to use what is a disadvantage to our advantage. So, in the films that we've done that are prephotographic—*The Shakers*, a good deal of it, and certainly *Thomas Jefferson,* and *Lewis and Clark*, we had to find new ways to tell stories, relying more and more on live cinematography.

Is your style of filmmaking—with voiceovers, studio shoots, archival material, and interviews—a response to cinema verité films?

No, not at all. In fact, the films that made the biggest impression on me were these unstructured, wild verité moments that we looked at in school. It's a very noble idea to capture the story on the fly without narration and without interviews, but I believe there's an inherent limitation to it. It's just not my style. I see really great verité films, but I have to work in a much more structured environment, and, I don't think, any less true.

But, you wouldn't disagree that your films are worlds apart from a cinema verité film?

Well, I remember Frederick Wiseman came to Hampshire College when I was just a snotty-nosed sophomore. I felt, he was incorrectly suggesting an objectivity to cinema verité films, and I objected. Now, I'm friends with Fred, and I don't think he remembers that I was this arrogant punk who was saying, these films aren't objective.

The bookend of this was being on a panel at the Telluride Film Festival a couple of years ago, about 2002, with D A Pennebaker, Chris Hegedus, Michael Moore, Steven Cantor, who just made a lovely film on Willie Nelson, Werner Herzog, and myself. At one point Michael Moore was talking and Werner interrupted him and said, "I'm interested in an ecstatic truth in my documentaries, in my films. Ken, here, is interested in an emotional truth. And you, with your big belly, are interested in a physical truth." And then he turned to D A and he said, "And you, I think we are enemies. Cinema verité is the cinema of accountants." To me, it was one of these stunning moments.

What happened next?

Everyone was so diplomatic. But I'll always remember that. And Werner *is* interested in an ecstatic, kind of poetic, operatic truth. I always describe myself as an emotional archeologist, uninterested in the dry dates and facts of the past. And for Michael Moore's cinema to be effective he injects himself into it with the same presence as a slapstick artist of feature films. He's in there, in your face, and it's all very much a part of his physical presence. It's very interesting. As to "the cinema of accountants," I don't want to touch that with a ten-foot pole.

Choosing an Awkward Process

Has your process changed over the years, as both research technology and your style have evolved?

In the beginning I did everything. Pre-Internet, I went to every archive, I shot every shot. I didn't do the interviews; cinematographer/coproducer Buddy Squires did the interviews. I wrote, and worked very closely with the writer.

Now, as I work with the same people over and over again, I'm obligated to give them more rope. So I'm sending people out. The Internet permits us to go out and collect the stuff where we are, so we're not going out and doing these mammoth road trips where we're visiting 160 archives of the Civil War, and putting up each image and shooting it individually.

You seem to prefer the old days, where you were more hands-on.

Well, there's a loss there, because you're not asking the curator, "What else do you have?" You've spent two days there, hanging out, and they're willing to bring out their favorites. Or you see something on the wall that's not germane, but it's just fantastic. We're not getting that many surprises, the way we used to, but we're getting access to the archives a lot quicker, through the Internet and through being able to download photographs, crudely digitize them, and work with them before we actually go and film originals.

But I think, for me, the process has gotten better now that I've allowed others to do so much more in producing. I mean, I'd love to do it, but it corresponds with

"Nobody's got a monopoly on the right decision."

a time in my life when I'm busy doing many, many other things, including raising money and promoting. Not that we never did that before, but it's really good to have a family.

"A Film by Ken Burns" is a collaboration, but you're making the final decisions.

The thing is, it's autocratic: Somebody has to be responsible for making the decision at the end of the day, and that person is me. But until that moment that you have to do it, it behooves me, and it's a better process, to be open to anybody. So, you can come in and sit in the editing room, and your opinion is as valued as anybody's. And if you're confused, that's hugely important to us. We love that sense of participation.

Before, I used to sit in the editing room every single day and choose the shots, but now I can trust others. They know how I think. And nobody's got a monopoly on the right decision. I'm the first to say, "Oh, that wasn't a good idea, let me try it this way." I think we've created an atmosphere where everybody feels that.

How did you arrive at your method of historical storytelling—bringing a photograph to life, with music, cinematography, narration, and sound effects?

We had adopted an approach in which we would treat an old photograph as if it were a live shot, and we treat a live shot as if it's a two-dimensional composed image. So, you go to an archive—say you're working on *The Civil War* and you're spending six weeks in the National Archives or the Library of Congress paper print collection—and there's Matthew Brady's collection, and we bring in an easel and two umbrella lights. We start at the beginning and we take photograph number one of thousands.

I put it up, and I look through the viewfinder, and I shoot—five shots, ten shots, two shots, whatever it is, looking, listening to the photographs. *Listening* to the photographs. Is that horse whinnying? Is that cannon firing? Are those trees rustling? Are those troops tramping? Is that water lapping? Is that bird cawing? Whatever it is. You trust it to come alive.

Ken Burns filming *Lewis and Clark* at Fort Clatsop, Oregon. "It is true that if my films are like photographs in a gallery, you could line them up on a wall and say they look more or less the same, but each individual film is so uniquely different from the others that style, in the end, just becomes a description of how one solves the problems of production."

Photo by Karl Maadam of The Daily Astorian. *Courtesy of Florentine Films.*

What about when you need to convey something literal, like a historical fact?

In another aspect of filming, we're out shooting something—a building, a bridge, a landscape—and we're trying to look for more formal considerations. The goal is to show its plasticity, its two-dimensionality, its compositional qualities. We're asking something that's two-dimensional to become three-dimensional, and we're asking something that's three-dimensional to become two-dimensional.

Music seems to be central to your films. Is that part of the research process?

We don't do the music at the end. We do the music at the beginning. We record, we identify many tunes before editing starts, or early in editing, go into the studio, and record dozens of versions of that tune. And then the rhythm and pacing of the music is organic to the editing process. It is, in fact, dictating the rhythm and pacing of our writing, sometimes. So, we're finding ourselves shortening a sentence or lengthening it to reach the end of a musical phrase. Rather than lock the picture, hand it over to somebody who's providing us not with jewels of tapestry, but wall-to-wall carpeting, which is merely attempting to amplify emotions we hope, we pray, are there. We know if they're there, because it's an organic process.

Do you think about the history and the script when selecting images from these vast archives? Tell me about your famous research process.

First of all, we never stop researching. There's no preproduction phase. Research goes on all the time. And it's not done by a legion of researchers, who are traditionally the lowest rung on a production company ladder, but by us. That is to say, the writers, the producers, the director, and maybe one or two other people closest to us, who've worked with us on a number of projects. We don't want to send somebody who's relatively uninitiated into a situation where they're at an archive with a 1000 photographs. And they may make a Xerox of 500 of them, but I won't see the others. It's not so much what you say yes to, it's what you say no to in the business of film; the negative space of creation.

You must have a high shooting ratio.

When you speak about a shooting ratio—that is to say, footage shot to footage used—you have to honor what is not used. These are not bad scenes. The proverbial cutting room floor is not filled with rubble. It's filled with the negative space of creation, that which you don't use. And there has to be a way to accurately honor that. One of the ways is to *not* put the most significant part of what you do, the discovery, on the shoulders of the least important person in a production hierarchy. The researcher should be the most important person. We never stop researching.

Why is that?

Because we wish to be incorrigible. Our process is different in many significant ways than what I can observe of that of my colleagues—with no pejorative implications. Others do preproduction, generate a script. The script is the bible from which they shoot, and it's the template from which they edit, and then they finish. Boom, done. It's no different from a widget that's produced in any other kind of industrial concern. Hollywood itself works to a large degree in this way. And they call it "the industry." I'm not involved in an industrial pursuit. I don't want to be involved in an industrial pursuit.

Can you give me an example of when you've continued the research well into postproduction?

Burns interviews the legendary baseball player Ted Williams, from the 18-hour PBS series, *Baseball*. "Baseball tells you about immigration. Each wave of immigrant groups sought this special status of citizenship conveyed not by the State Department but by participation in the national pastime. This is about the exclusion of women, about the growth and decay and rebirth of cities. It's about popular culture and advertising. It's about labor and management. So, all of a sudden I realize, 'Oh my God, I'm working on the sequel to *The Civil War.*'"

Photo by Joe Gosen for General Motors. Courtesy of Florentine Films.

I took a day off one weekend last winter, after we'd locked the film on Jack Johnson, and I was in an antique show in Manhattan. This guy was selling furniture and still photographs. One of them was a picture of white people who dressed up a baby in a wagon that was made to look like a boxing ring, and it said "Great White Hope— age 7 months." It was just these white people vibrating crazily about Jack Johnson. I bought it and put it into the film. Unlocked the film and put it in.

If research is ongoing, when do you begin writing?

Well, we will research throughout; we will shoot almost immediately, shooting what we're drawn to visually. And at the same time, as if the left hand doesn't know what the right hand is doing, we're also writing, unconcerned with whether there are images to, quote, illustrate, unquote, these scenes—because we want to avoid illustration.

Why?

Illustration is the thing that keeps it running at a rather superficial level. We're looking for—to borrow a term from still photography—*equivalencies* that resonate at many different levels. So we want to be able to write unfettered by some visual concern, and we want to shoot unfettered by somebody saying, "Well, that's not in the script." It makes the reconciliation incredibly difficult, but that's what we choose to do; an awkward process.

Wynton Marsalis, from *Jazz*. "In New Orleans, a band would march down the street; everybody heard the music. If you were white, green, red, it didn't make a difference. You were going to hear some swinging jazz music. The radio did that nationally because the airwaves were not segregated and could not be segregated."

Photo courtesy of Florentine Films.

When do you enter the cutting room?

Editing begins four or five drafts into a script.

Where does fact-checking enter in?

The drafts get redone by historical consulting, by our own rewriting, by the discovery of new materials, and by the addition of talking heads.

You're shooting interviews at the same time that you're continuing archival research, and the script is constantly being revised based on what surfaces from the shoot?

Yes. Because we want to go and ask questions of a talking head, unconcerned whether they're trying to get us from point A to point B on page 23 of a developing script. We don't want them to have to talk as if we've got images that we want them to speak to. We want them, who they *are*. They never see the questions in advance, so every talking head in any film I've made is a happy accident of trial and error. That's significantly different then most documentary approaches.

Typically, the entire script will be rewritten two, three, four, five, or ten times during the course of editing as we discover things. And we do discover things.

What is gained by this "awkward process"?

Rather than being that old forum, of a kind of didactic essayistic presentation of what I know, this is a sharing with the audience of what I've discovered. What we've discovered. And that, I think, makes the difference between how people receive it and what the popularity of a film is.

Ambitious Histories

You've produced three epic series for PBS—*The Civil War, Baseball,* and *Jazz*—that total more than 49 hours. You've told me before that they are all interconnected. Can you explain how?

I see them as a trilogy. As much as I'd like to claim that it had some sort of intentionality to its order, it was completely random. The first several films that I made, on the Brooklyn Bridge, the history of the Shakers religious sect, the Statue of Liberty, Huey Long, and the Congress, were all just chosen, as most of the projects are, randomly and haphazardly, without a game plan. After they were made, I began to notice that each of these subjects, as diverse as they are, seem to have as one determining factor hanging over them, the Civil War:

- The Brooklyn Bridge would not have been built without this new metal called steel, which the Civil War helped to promote. The man who built the Brooklyn Bridge, Washington Roebling, got his practical training as a bridge builder during the Civil War.

- The Shakers would not have declined so precipitously, not just for the economic and social changes that took place in America after the Civil War, but because of the psychic changes that took place in a country that had just murdered 630,000 of its own people.

- The Statue of Liberty was originally intended as a gift from the French to Mrs. Lincoln to commemorate the survival of the Union despite her husband's ultimate sacrifice, and only later became the symbol of immigration that we identity it with today.

- Huey Long came from a dirt poor North Louisiana parish that refused to secede from the Union. They thought the Confederacy was a rich man's cause. And so Winn Parish became this hotbed of radicalism and populism and socialism that eventually spawned Huey Long.

- And the Congress had its greatest test when there were two Congresses—one in Washington, D.C., and the other in Montgomery, Alabama, and later Richmond, Virginia.

So, everywhere I turned, the Civil War was there. I felt, I now have to do it. And since I'd been practicing and practicing on still photographs and first-person voices, in addition to the third-person narration, I had to take on what was one of the greatest challenges of my life.

The Civil War was the highest rated series in the history of PBS. It attracted an audience of 40 million during its premiere alone. Columnist George Will said, "If better use has ever been made of television, I have not seen it and do not expect to see better until Ken Burns turns his prodigious talents to his next project."

You won more than 40 major film and television awards for that series. So, based on that success, you went right into the 18-hour series, *Baseball*?

Well, even as I began it, I knew that after the Civil War I was going to do a short little valentine to baseball.

An 18-hour valentine?

When we started, I thought I knew a little bit about baseball. But I quickly found out how little I knew.

Why make a series about baseball?

Well, I had no idea, until I began it, that it was the sequel to *The Civil War*, insofar as everything you want to know about what the Civil War made us, describes the Civil War as the crossroads of our being. So the question is, *what did we become*?

You can learn not just from the age-old, familiar, political military narrative but by this so-called national pastime. The first progress in civil rights after the Civil War? Jackie Robinson. Why did the Civil War happen? Race. So they're connected. Baseball tells you about immigration. Each wave of immigrant groups sought this special status of citizenship conveyed not by the State Department but by participation in the national pastime. This is about the exclusion of women, about the growth and decay and rebirth of cities. It's about popular culture and advertising. It's about labor and management. So, all of a sudden I realize, "Oh my God, I'm working on the sequel to *The Civil War*."

"I had to take on what was one of the greatest challenges of my life."

It didn't start out as a series?

I think originally we were talking about two hours, but very quickly it's going to be five one-hours, then it's going to be nine one-hours, and all of a sudden it was 18 and a half hours long. It was longer than the Civil War series, because it was covering so much territory.

At what point did you draw all these connections between the subjects of your films?

One of the interviews that we did for the baseball series was with a man named Gerald Early, who is an African American scholar and writer in St. Louis. And he says that when they study our American civilization 2000 years from now—and 2000 years is a long, long time—Americans will be known for only three things: the Constitution, baseball, and jazz music. He said they're the three most beautiful things Americans have ever invented.

And I realized I'd just made a film on the Constitution's greatest test, the Civil War, and it suffused every film I worked on. I was in the middle of working on the history of baseball. I was obligated to go into something I knew nothing about. I had to take on jazz.

Do you feel the same way about the biographies you've directed? Compelled to do them?

Well, all biographies, all efforts, are essentially failures in this way. You can only still show, in the end, what you don't know. I mean, biography is a constituent building log of all of the major films. It is ultimately, if you're honest, a failing enterprise—because we don't even know the people closest to us, our family members, our loved ones. It's impossible to know anybody. But the effort is what propels the human adventure, whether it's filmmaking or art or politics or religion.

What motivates you to take on these enormous, ambitious series?

Essentially all of the projects are born out of a deep enthusiasm for the subject matter, and the mystery of the subject matter. Not the fact that I get it, but that I want to get it, or that I'm trying to get it.

First-Person, Bottom-Up History

The sources you use to tell the story in your films range from historical experts to everyday citizens' diaries and letters. How does drawing from a diverse range of voices contribute to the authenticity of your films?

Well, I think you almost have to take a step back from that question and address the one of objectivity and subjectivity. I think in the first day of film class everybody ought to just completely forget about objectivity. God is objective, and She is not telling us.

So each form of film is an attempt to organize the chaos that is life: the universe. I think we come to a kind of shorthand that fiction is narrative and untrue, and that

documentaries are true and objective. And that's not true. We know from literature that some of the greatest truths emerge from fiction, and that it's possible for a
fiction film to carry incredible amounts of truth.

I work in a medium—documentary—that's interested in fact-based drama, fact-
based narrative, and that's a huge difference. I think what makes the documentary
a kind of lesser animal, in the scale of things, is that for too long it was a didactic,
essayistic thing; an expression of someone else's already-arrived-at ends, and not
interested in narrative. The same Aristotelian principals that guide a feature film
guide what I do.

**Does your approach of using different types of sources lends the narrative
credibility?**

Our medium is so richly panned for being superficial. And in many cases that's a
deserved thing, as opposed to, say, a scholarly book on the subject. But a scholarly
book on the subject operates under many more laws than a documentary film, and
it's often very narrow. It can subscribe, for example, only to the current fashion in
the academy at that moment—Marxism, Deconstruction, semiotics, gender studies, and everything has to be filtered through that.

We have the ability in our films to, in the case of history, have a diversity of per-
spectives. One of the most important things to me has been doing history from the
bottom up, and not just the top down. To not only be interested in what Lincoln
said, but what the ordinary person said. And I've done that in almost every film.
So to me, the past comes alive when you're aware of how ordinary people spoke.
What women were doing. What minorities were doing. What labor was doing.
What people were doing who have always been on the short end of what stands for
conventional history. Conventional history is essentially rich and powerful politicians and military people. And I reject that.

On political grounds?

On all grounds. Certainly on political grounds, but also on social and, in the end,
truth grounds. Because how could you possibly know an age if the only person

you knew was Abraham Lincoln? Now, I happen to think Abraham Lincoln was the most important person in American history, and I will defend that view until I run out of breath. But at the same time, I think Abraham Lincoln is set in even more spectacular relief by (A) knowing ordinary people from that time were doing extraordinary things, like fighting in his war, and (B) knowing his faults as well, which is another very important part of the question—do you accept a sanitized Madison Avenue version of history, or do you manipulate history to make it serve your propagandistic intent, or do you take a much more risky stance, it seems to me, and embrace whatever it is that you find? How do you do that, without filtering out stuff? Bottom-up as well as top-down history, and history with all its warts. That's really important to me.

You discover unconventional history from everyday people, and then you often cast celebrities to read the voiceover of everyday citizens' diaries and letters. Why?

First of all, I don't cast celebrity, I cast talent. So there are people in my films that are from our little village in New Hampshire, where I live, and friends, and voices that I like. People who are in my films are extremely talented people who also happen to be, in many cases, celebrities. So that poses a problem. We all know the documentary films where there's a cast that you're totally distracted by, "Oh, isn't that Arnold Schwarzenegger reading the thing?" I don't choose people that way. I choose them so if you're sort of hyperaware you might say, "Oh, that's Ed Harris," or "That's Samuel L. Jackson." But mostly, you're struggling to hear what they say. These people are so good they inhabit the words.

A hallmark of my style is not just a third-person narrator, but something I pioneered, which is a chorus of voices speaking many different things from the past—first-person voices. And it's very important to me that if I'm going to use them, they can't call attention to themselves. They've got to inhabit the love letter, the newspaper dispatch, the military account, whatever it is.

When do you start thinking about character development? How does that fit into the construction of the narrative?

the arc of your narrative."

That is a great question. I start thinking about characters right away, because biography is the constituent building block, I believe, of narrative. That's just a choice I've made. You need to be communicating about the lives of other people all the time, and that becomes the bricks. There's other mortar, but characters are the bricks of making a narrative. Development is another thing altogether, because the hardest thing to do well in narrative film is character development. So they're not just one-dimensional. And in history, you have both an advantage and a disadvantage. That is to say, you cannot manipulate character development to fit into the arc of your narrative, but at the same time, the character development is a given because you know what happens to that person.

So what you look for becomes a question of how you investigate history. What are the questions you ask? Are you interested, say, in an artist like Frank Lloyd Wright, the psychological and the personal as well as the professional and the artistic? Because I would suggest that his troubled relationship with his families, his clients and his friends speaks to who he is as an artistic genius. Now, it's easier to just focus on the artistic genius and live on that in an essayistic way. Or we can try to do a biography that's complicated enough to blend the personal and the professional, which is what we try to do. And, I think, give a much richer sense of who the person is.

Taking Creative Risks

We've discussed how your style has become recognizable, but in the beginning was it developed from experimentation?

Absolutely. It's going to take a lot of trial and error before anything really works out. There were myriad problems and techniques that we had to resolve. How to photograph still photographs was a big question in the very beginning. Just the notion of how you would rephotograph much more energetically than had been done before. Also, combining complicated sound effects tracks.

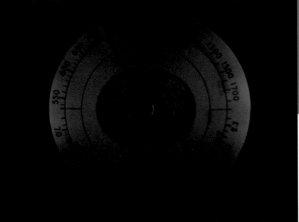

From *Empire of the Air*. Burns says, "We realized that radio is this incredibly active medium. You're the director—in your imagination. You're the cinematographer—in your imagination. You're the costume designer—in your imagination. You hear these words or the music or the sound effects, and you create everything else. It's a hugely participatory thing."

Photos courtesy of Florentine Films.

Tell me about your creative use of sound. You used some novel approaches on *The Civil War,* including original sound effects. Why was that creative choice important?

In retrospect it seems so small and insignificant, but it was monumental for us. The unwritten rule of documentaries is that when you cut away, when you cut to a talking head—for example, we're in the middle of a battle—they cut out the effects. And as I was watching it, I'm going, something is wrong here, I want to be *in* this battle. The whole idea to tell history is to place people in the moment. So I said, run the battle sound effects with the image of the interview.

One of the editors said, "I don't think we should do that," as if that was bad, that there was some god or ethic of documentary that precluded that. And I said, "No, no, no, watch!" So we ran the effects on the show. People are talking about the Battle of Shiloh and it was, like, whoa! Because suddenly they put us there. And we have done that ever since.

But it was difficult for you to take risks, to defy convention.

For us, at the time, it was a huge, tortured decision. I remember waking up at 4 a.m. the next morning—was this right? Was there a god and ethic of documentary that would come down and smite us? Now, it might, in another documentary form, seem untrue to do that. But we were trying to create a reality where the past was present. Faulkner once said, "History is not was, but *is*." And we were looking for those *is* moments. One of the ways we did it was to try that. And it worked. Suddenly there was an organic unit of this thing, and it wasn't just dead silence, the voice, and then back to the battle. But you felt like the interview subject was watching from behind a tree, or that you were watching from behind a tree. That was great.

Tell me about how you used sound in the opening of your film *Empire of the Air*. It's one of my favorite film openings because you place the viewer in the time period immediately. Can you describe how that developed?

Empire of the Air is about the early pioneers of radio. Not the golden age stars, but this very dark backstage drama; the three men most responsible for radio's growth and development, David Sarnoff, Lee de Forest, and Edwin Howard Armstrong.

We realized that radio is this incredibly active medium. That is to say, you're the director—in your imagination. You're the cinematographer—in your imagination. You're the costume designer—in your imagination. You hear these words or the music or the sound effects, and you create everything else. It's a hugely participatory thing. And a lot of it has to do with the absence of imagery.

So we began to work on a variation of something I'd experienced a little bit in my film on Thomas Hart Benton, when I was trying to focus on his style of painting. The problem there was how to *see* a painting rather than in a frame. I was into microscopically examining the context of it; the contours of the landscape of the painting fading in and out. And in *The Civil War,* in order to rivet people's attention on some of the dead at Gettysburg, we began to fade in and out on the bodies, and wake you up with what's going on. It was a way of focusing attention. I realized that in *Empire of the Air*, we could begin to suggest that imagination that takes place, that active imagination that takes place, when there are no images. So for periods of time in the introduction, it just fades to black. And you hear information. You certainly hear music and sound effects. But *nothing's there*, which is, of course, terrifying for a filmmaker, who's all about always supplying an image, and certainly terrifying to the powers that be. It made everybody anxious. But I think to varying degrees of success in that film, it does rivet your attention. And that was our intention.

Style is communicating subject matter.

Well, the problem—not pejorative—is how do you give watchers an idea of what it was like to just be a listener. The style, the accumulation of techniques we use to try to deal with that problem, is this idea of taking away pictures for an extended period of time and asking you to hold in darkness.

Fund-raising and PBS

How did you finance your first film projects?

In the beginning, we patched together patchwork quilts of funders from corporations to government granting agencies to private foundations to individuals to state tourism boards. And it's still that kind of hodgepodge of funding every time we go out.

But eventually you found your home on PBS.

Twenty-five years ago, what we managed to do was back our way into public television. And I say back our way, but now I'm incredibly happy.

Your original goal wasn't to show your work on public television?

Originally, I assumed, like most documentary filmmakers, that I made films that would be shown at festivals, maybe get some cable distribution. But so many of the sources of funding that were willing to give us money, like the National Endowment for the Humanities and the Corporation for Public Broadcasting, and even private corporations and foundations, expected us to *give* the film to public television. So there was a bit of a bargain that was struck which was, I will take this money knowing that this film won't be sold at the end, it will just be given to public television. But, in the end, the calculus was exactly right.

Your funding always comes from nonprofit sources, why?

Because the type of work we do is so labor intensive, it takes so much time, that it means you can't just max out your credit card and shoot a few interviews and edit it. These are massive things that take years to do, and you're either going to starve or you're going to do it.

You prefer to have your work on television, instead of in theaters. Why are you happy with your home on PBS?

Because rather than being seen by a few hundred people at a film festival, or a few thousand, and maybe tens of thousands on a cable outlet, these films are being seen by millions of people. I thought that if you had a certain passion to do something, if you brought an enthusiasm to its production, and if you were answering questions about what happened in history, then the resulting film shouldn't be only for people with a particular set of beliefs. It should be for everybody. You should be directing it at an ignorant but curious person. That is to say, they are ignorant of the subject you're covering. And, "may I entertain you?"

What's the relationship between moving forward on a project and raising the funds necessary to produce it? Do you wait for all the funding to come in prior to starting?

"All along I've had a perhaps naïve faith in my own ability to do it."

Well, all along I've had a perhaps naïve faith in my own ability to do it. So whenever I felt in my heart that I wanted to do a project, we've done it. And if I'm raising money even after it's done—which I'm doing now for *Jack Johnson*, because of the delicacy and the controversy of the subject—because we're over budget, so be it.

What happens when the funding is not coming together?

I've had some projects that have been fully funded before I began, but in most cases, 90 percent of the cases, I've been constantly fund-raising while I'm making it. And I feel very lucky, because I've been able to push through that.

You have a unique relationship with PBS at this point. Tell me about it.

I know that not every filmmaker feels positive about PBS. Some of them feel that it's a kind of impenetrable arcane fortress and you've got to know the secret handshake or whatever. I haven't found that to be true, but I know others have felt that.

It's perfect for me. I came into it accidentally, because my films had to be given to public television. I figured out how it worked, and ultimately chose a station that leaves me alone. And they don't tell me to change something. They don't ask me to soft-pedal the issues that I bring up; I'm very passionate about race and almost every film ends up being a fairly complicated, sometimes controversial discussion of race. They are excited to have the films, and I feel the same way about them.

And it doesn't have the pitfalls of the other venues, which are the loss of ownership and creative controls. At the end of every film, I own them. No one's told me how to make it. And I can say, as I said before, that if you don't like it, it's all my fault. That's the way I want it to be. I don't want to be able to sit here and say, "Well, you know, they didn't give me enough money, they wouldn't let me shoot this scene, they made me use this narrator, they made me use this actor."

◀ **"In film classes back in college, we debated endlessly whether films ever really made people do something. Shortly after _Brooklyn Bridge_ first appeared, _The New York Times_ ran a front-page photograph of a married couple and their children walking over the Brooklyn Bridge. They said they were from Idaho and they had traveled all the way to New York so their family could see first-hand this remarkable structure. They said they got the idea after watching a film on PBS."**
—Ken Burns, from the PBS website.

Photo courtesy of Florentine Films.

So as long as you finance your work through foundations, PBS gives you total creative freedom?

Completely. They're great, if you're good. And that's important. I think what we've been able to do with PBS, is that the decisions we have made have been all based on what's best for the film—with regard to time, length of programs, nonstandard length. How long we take to do them, waiting for the right image, choosing, perhaps, to continue to edit linearly, or whatever it is. I'm not saying that these are hugely outrageous budgets, but it's all on the screen. No big overhead for us.

What advice do you have for filmmakers?

Have something to say. When students ask, "How do you do it?" I say, "There's two things, and you're going to despise me for the platitudes that they are, first, but you've got to know who you are—because we've seen so many people drawn to film for some perceived glamour that isn't there. And it's no shame to say, "You know what? I don't have something to say." Because a few of us do, and we're very lucky, or we're burdened—cursed. But whatever it is, if you have something to say, then you can still do that.

The other thing is perseverance. Because I've rarely run into bad filmmakers, I rarely run into bad ideas. So it means that everyone's got to work that much harder just to make sure it happens. You must overcome not just the obstacles in production, but all the other obstacles. Not enough money, a government not disposed to funding documentary films, competition and mean-spiritedness within the community. All of these things have to be overcome.

Even now, at this stage in your career, it requires perseverance?

I had, on my desk, for I don't know how many years, two large three-ring binders filled with every rejection I got for my first film, *Brooklyn Bridge*. There's never been a moment where I haven't, on any given day of the year, been actively pursuing the raising of money to pay for these things. It didn't get any easier as my success grew or the popularity of the films grew. Mainly, I think, because we also took on more projects. Or they got bigger. Sometimes there's a backlash—"Oh, well, he should be able to do it. Let's give the money to the next person," which is a perfectly reasonable triage to perform in a world that has many good filmmakers and many good ideas and very little money.

Process and Pragmatism

I understand your films and series take years to make, and yet you work with a very specific team of collaborators who also work independently. How does that work, practically? When do you crew up?

We're usually talking about it years in advance. Even from the beginning.

I just finished a film called *Unforgivable Blackness: The Rise and Fall of Jack Johnson*. We were talking about doing this in 1992, and we knew, more or less, three-quarters of the four principal people involved. We knew who the writer would be; we knew that I would direct it and coproduce it; and I knew one of the coproducers. And it was four years ago that I picked Paul Barnes, who's my long-time editor, to be the other coproducer, the third coproducer. We have less of a civilized circumstance, the model of a corporation, and more of a heroic one—that is to say, we're grabbing from the filmmaking family that we've worked with for years. Then, we constantly turn over a fresh bunch of young people who come and work for us, first as unpaid interns. Those who show a lot of promise move in and through the ranks. Some leave right away and take jobs in Hollywood, commercial businesses. Others stay.

Do you ever feel deadline pressure?

No. We've been very lucky over the last 25 or 30 years that the projects we've chosen, we've been realistic about how long it takes. And we have met every self-imposed deadline. No one's imposed a deadline on us. So we've been estimating even six or seven years out on a film that we're doing. *Jazz* took six and a half years to make. With the decision to make it, it was seven years out. And I knew that it would be broadcast more or less when it was.

"It's terrifying to make these films."

Why is delivering well before the broadcast date important to you?

I know many people who are mixing just a few weeks from broadcast. But we're done six months before it's broadcast, at least, so that a hugely important and often neglected part of this—what I call the evangelism—can take place. It's a phenomenological question: With so many channels you can make a great film that nobody sees, so you have to go out and sing about it.

How do you remain inspired by the topic three years into a seven-year project?

Everybody asks that, but by the end of the film, I'm more excited than I was at the beginning. I'm more excited about *Jack Johnson* now because, when I started, I didn't realize that this was not just a film about athletic accomplishment and race, but about sex, freedom, and who we are. People always tell me, "I work on these deadlines, we turn out a film in six months, you did this for six years? You must get bored." And I say, "Never." It's this escalating sense of challenge, and escalating sense of terror.

So it's entirely enjoyable for you.

I feel so lucky. I feel like I have the best job in the country. I mean, they're paying me to do this. How is this possible?

Many documentary makers I've spoken with find their work rewarding, but they speak about sacrifice, and the endless challenges.

Maybe I've been unfair in describing this all in these perfect conditions. It's terrifying to make these films. This is such a huge thing. I remember when I decided to do *The Civil War*, my father said, "What part?" I said, "All of it." And he just walked out of the room shaking his head, like, "Oh, my son is an idiot." But I paid for that decision every morning at 4 a.m. for five years, and guess what? I still wake up at 4 a.m. going, "How do I do this?"

We're in the middle of working on a massive history of experiences of everyday Americans during the Second World War, and we're trying to figure out how to connect several different towns. It's this three-dimensional chess puzzle, and it just wakes me up. So, I think we're galvanized by the sheer terror of what we do. Because you have to get it right, have to figure out how to do it. I think that terror and the love combine in a very interesting way. They don't cancel each other out! The love comes when it comes, and the terror is always there.

Have you endured sacrifices to make your films?

When I started, for years and years and years I didn't make more than $2500 or $3000 a year for 1978, '79, '80, '81. I moved out of New York to New Hampshire, so I could live for nothing and make my films. I did! I just thought, if I become a documentary filmmaker I'm going to take a vow of anonymity and poverty.

Well, that didn't work out.

It didn't work out, I'm very happy to say! I just had a conversation on the subway a few minutes ago with a woman who'd seen the film and wanted to talk about it. It's just great.

I noticed when I came into this restaurant, people recognized you. Do you often get stopped on the street?

Every day. A hundred times a day. And I'm thinking, wait a second, I'm glad I still live in New Hampshire. This little village where I live, all of whatever notoriety I have, plus 50 cents, gets me a cup of coffee. They don't care. The roads have to be plowed in the winter.

Keeps you human.

Oh, it does. That and having daughters. My most important production. Coproduction.

Errol
Morris

...and whoop the hell out of 'em.
Kill some of'em,
that's what I want to do.

Director

Revealing Unexpected Realities

WITHIN THE ENTERTAINMENT INDUSTRY, ERROL MORRIS HOLDS a chameleon position. To the commercial production world, he's established as a highly successful director, both innovative and intelligent. (He's one of the only, if not *the* only, director of TV commercials who has written an opinion-page article published in *The New York Times*.) Within talent and advertising agencies, he is known for his exceptional off-kilter vision, and honored in ways usually reserved for noncommercial artists. (In November 1999, his work received a full retrospective at the Museum of Modern Art. In 2002, the organizers of the Academy Awards asked him to direct the short film that introduced the annual Oscars ceremony; it featured a series of real-life characters—some well-known, some everyday citizens—describing their passion for movies.) In a 2004 *Adweek* article honoring Morris's contributions as someone who "rises above the fray to create work that resonates and inspires," Weiden and Kennedy producer Jesse

Errol Morris filmography

Director

The Fog of War: Eleven Lessons from the Life of Robert S. McNamara (2003)

First Person (2000)

Mr. Death: The Rise and Fall of Fred A. Leuchter Jr. (1999)

Fast, Cheap & Out of Control (1997)

The Dark Wind (1991)

A Brief History of Time (1991)

The Thin Blue Line (1988)

Vernon, Florida (1981)

Gates of Heaven (1978)

Producer

The Fog of War: Eleven Lessons from the Life of Robert S. McNamara (2003)

First Person (2000)

Film critic Roger Ebert says, "After 20 years of reviewing films, I haven't found another filmmaker who intrigues me more. Errol Morris is like a magician, and as great a filmmaker as Hitchcock or Fellini."

Photo courtesy of Errol Morris.

Wann said Morris has a talent for "finding things in the moment. He's not a storyboarder. He has a certain unusual eye, and you see it in the stylized sequences of his films and his commercials." In fact, his commercial work includes several of the best-known television campaigns: a venerated post-9/11 campaign for United Airlines; the famous Apple Computer "Switch" campaign; a corresponding testimonial-style campaign for MoveOn.org, featuring voters who voted for Bush in the prior election but planned to cast their votes for Kerry in 2004; an Emmy Award-winning commercial ("Photo Booth") for PBS; Miller High Life's popular "anti-beer beer commercials," and countless others for ESPN, American Express, and Intel.

But to the documentary world, Morris is firmly planted among the ranks of feature-length documentary makers. He makes the directorial shortlist of any nonfiction theatrical, television, or festival programmer. Morris tells me, "Last month I ran into a filmmaker in L.A. who said, 'I love your work.' I asked him which films he liked and he said, 'The ones you did for Miller High Life.' No one in the commercial world even knows I *make* documentaries, and vice versa!" That perception gap says more about both Morris's versatility and unusual productivity in two seemingly disparate arenas than it does about his stature in either. In fact, the balance between commercial spot and long-form documentary work provides what he sees as "cross-pollination" between the forms, one that contributes to his ongoing innovativeness in both arenas.

One example of how Morris has come up with original solutions to fundamental creative filmmaking problems—across all his productions—is found within a key narrative component: the standard interview. In films such as 1997's *Fast, Cheap & Out of Control* or 2003 Oscar winner *The Fog of War: Eleven Lessons from the Life of Robert S. McNamara*, Morris has taken the uninspired talking-head interview and transformed it. To conduct his interviews, he invented a piece of equipment he calls the Interrotron, which is described by his company as "a modified TelePrompTer … that allows Morris to project his image on a monitor placed directly over the camera's lens. Interviewees address Morris's image on the monitor while looking directly at the camera." So, rather than looking off camera to converse directly with the interviewer and indirectly with the audience, the

Mr. Death: The Rise and Fall of Fred A.
Leuchter Jr. (1999)
Fast, Cheap, and Out of Control
(1997)
Vernon, Florida (1981)
Gates of Heaven (1978)

Editor
Gates of Heaven (1978)

Writer
The Thin Blue Line (1988)

Interrotron allows both Morris (the interviewer) and the audience to make eye contact with his interview subjects. The resulting footage enhances the intensity of the interviewees' answers; the intimacy of many of these exchanges is unsurpassed. "It's the difference between faux first person and the true first person," says Morris. "The Interrotron inaugurates the birth of true first-person cinema."

To that end—the pursuit of lush, well-crafted, cinematic documentary—he has employed many original approaches to the form, including the creative use of historical audio recordings running behind both original live action and rare archival film footage. Furthermore, the visuals are brought to life with abstract closeups, unusual cuts, and bold color-correction treatments. All of his films draw upon the best in fine art and film history, as Morris develops his story lines with extremely high production values, photography, and strong, hypnotic scores, many by Phillip Glass. In watching his films one comes away with a sense that this is a director who aims high—and is seeking something *more*: beyond the development of his own prolific body of work towards a larger ambition. Perhaps he hopes to supplant the low-budget reputation of documentary film—born out of photo and news journalism—with high culture panache, to raise the bar for the medium.

In content selection as well as in form, Morris pursues avenues of the weird and wonderful. He has been determined to follow the beat of his own drum from the very beginning, always seeking eccentric real-life characters. In 1978, he was inspired to direct his first nonfiction feature after discovering a headline in the *San Francisco Chronicle*: "450 Dead Pets To Go To Napa." The resulting documentary, *Gates of Heaven,* follows the surreal startup story of two entrepreneurs—through the launch of two competing pet cemeteries—and makes for an entertaining, rich, and wry commentary on American culture and capitalism.

His second documentary, *Vernon, Florida*, as originally conceived featured the residents of a Florida town who made their income by undergoing radical self-mutilation and filing for compensation through an insurance fraud scam. In discussing the film, Morris observes, "They literally became a fraction of themselves to become whole financially." Outside of these residents's highly bizarre mind-set, the most unusual aspect of Morris's filmmaking is his careful narrative tone:

accepting of the truly peculiar events he records, while simultaneously commenting on them. Regardless of his caution, some subjects prove too provocative and sensitive for exposure. According to Morris's production company, the insurance fraud film had to be reimagined when "his subjects threatened to murder him. Forced to come up with a new concept, he created *Vernon, Florida*, about the unconventional residents of a Southern swamp town." Even with its less litigious focus, *Vernon, Florida*—like all of Morris's films—features unforgettable characters. In *Gates of Heaven,* one elderly woman has taught her poodle to sing. Viewing this scene, one cannot help but become transfixed: As they sit in her kitchen, after parroting her voice, the poodle joins the woman to perform a duet. To watch a Morris documentary is to enter a dreamlike reality.

The Thin Blue Line

The Thin Blue Line, released in 1988, took up the case of Randall Adams, who was wrongly convicted for murder in Dallas County, Texas. The film, and Morris's investigation of the case, is credited with Adams's conviction being overturned.

In *The Thin Blue Line* you combined traditional interviews with Philip Glass's mesmerizing score, and then used 35mm film and commercial cinematography to illustrate and reillustrate the different characters's contradictory versions of what happened the night of the murder. It's a very controlled approach to the documentary form. Many of your visual techniques—such as the theatrical reenactment—which are used frequently in nonfiction television today, were first conceived of in this film.

What was the reaction when it first came out?

When *The Thin Blue Line* came out, the use of reenactments was considered heretical. The movie was endlessly criticized, and then endlessly *imitated!* People see it today and they say, "Well, what is so unusual about this? I see this everywhere." Well, yes, it is everywhere, but it wasn't everywhere when *The Thin Blue Line* was made!

Did you have a clear vision of the final film before you started? Was using Glass's music, and stylish reenactments to illustrate the flaws in the eyewitness testimony, part of your initial concept?

No. *The Thin Blue Line* is a perfect example of a movie that found itself as it was being put together. It was started with an entirely different project in mind. I knew nothing about Randall Adams, nothing about David Harris. In fact, *no one* knew anything about Randall Adams or David Harris. For all intents and purpose, this was a closed case. It had been solved to almost everybody's satisfaction. Randall Adams had been tried and convicted and sentenced to death for the murder of Dallas police officer Robert Wood. And that was that. There were a few scattered people who felt that there had been a miscarriage of justice, but they were very few and far between. I stumbled on the case purely by accident.

How did you meet Randall Adams?

I was planning to make a movie about a Dallas psychiatrist, and had started the movie. And at the suggestion of Dr. James Grigson [featured in the original concept for the film] I went and interviewed over a dozen people that he had helped put on death row. Randall Adams was one of them. And the intention, of course, was not to uncover miscarriages of justice; the intention was just to interview, as Dr. Grigson described them, "cold-blooded killers" who are, quote unquote, "different than you me."

You weren't looking to tell Adams's story—a failure of the justice system.

No. To illustrate some of the things that Grigson was saying, I met Randall Adams again. I picked a dozen or so names, but the choice of those names was random. It could have been another dozen or so. Grigson had been responsible for putting 30, 40, 50 people on death row. So I read about the other stories as well, but as I read about Adams's story I slowly but surely became convinced that there had been a terrible miscarriage of justice. And then the movie changed. It was no longer a movie of Dr. Grigson. It was a movie about Randall Adams. It was *The Thin Blue Line.*

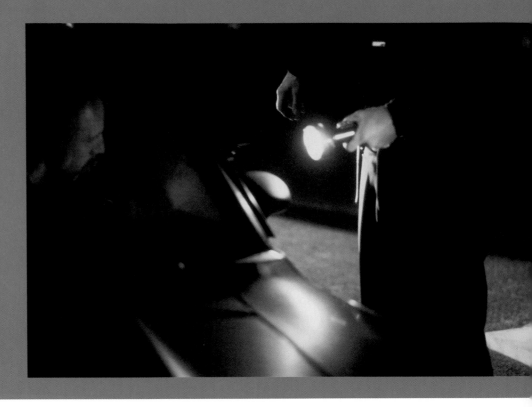

Images from *The Thin Blue Line*. Morris says, "Whether it's interviews, or reenactments that bring you deeper into the mystery of what happened, or graphics that stress certain aspects of the story ... or the strange mystery of Randall Adams, whose incomplete so-called confession was no confession at all, it's designed to take you into the story in a powerful and dramatic way."

Photo courtesy of Miramax Films.

After you stopped filming your original concept about Dr. Grigson, and decided to start from scratch and focus on Randall Adams, how long did the filmmaking process take?

Well, when I met Adams, that was the beginning of over a year and a half, close to two years, of tracking people down, interviewing them, of doing research. I've pointed out many times, I believe this is true. You don't always know about the claims you make on behalf of yourself.

Aside from the stylistic innovation, what makes *The Thin Blue Line* a film that so many filmmakers refer to for inspiration?

Well, *The Thin Blue Line* is unusual. It may even be unique. It's not telling the story about a murder case, it's not *about* an investigation. It *is* an investigation! The investigation was done, in part, with a camera—culminating with David Harris's confession to me. It was on tape—following the malfunctioning of my camera in my interview with him—the tape on which he essentially confesses to the murder!

"What's interesting is, in *The Thin Blue Line* the reenactments are never purported to show you what really happened. They weren't a way of illustrating reality. They were telling you something quite different, that reality often is ineluctable. That it's very hard to grab ahold of. The visuals are ironic in a very dramatic sense. They're illustrations of untruths. They're not dramatic reenactments of reality. They're dramatic reenactments of unreality."

Photo courtesy of Miramax Films.

I read all the time that *The Thin Blue Line* is the movie that got an innocent man out of prison, saved an innocent man from death row. But what's forgotten is that it's the movie *and* the investigation that did it.

You were a filmmaker, and a detective. How did your approach allow that to happen?

The material I uncovered in the interviews was investigative in nature. Interviews often take the form of a set of questions that people ask, and they already know the answers that they're looking for. They are not investigative. And I try very, very hard to make the interviews that I do something other than about the things that I want to hear, or expect to hear, or think I'm going to hear. I try to be at least open to the possibility that something unexpected is going to happen. And that was certainly true in *The Thin Blue Line*. It's an investigation I'm very, very proud of. I'm proud of the movie, I'm even prouder of the investigation.

You said earlier that you started to discover "slowly but surely" when you were talking to Adams and Harris that there had been a miscarriage of justice. What tipped you off that perhaps the wrong man was in prison?

Randall Adams, of course, told me he was innocent, but, of course, I didn't believe him. The first red flag was when I went to Austin. By statute every capital murder trial in Texas is appealed to the Texas Court of Criminal Appeals. You can go to that court, and in the basement they have the transcripts of every capital murder trial. You can sit there, and you can read. And I was reading. I could see the frame but I couldn't see the picture, and that was true of the transcript. There was something wrong with that story.

Why did you sense the story was wrong?

It all centered on David Harris, on the star prosecution witness who *claimed* to be in the passenger's seat of the car, and to have observed at close range Randall Adams's murder of Robert Wood. There was just something wrong with it. Then I started to uncover more and more material about David Harris. And as more and more stuff accumulated, it became clear that I was dealing with a guy with an incredible history of violence—particularly to authority figures.

He had tried to kill his commanding officer in the army. He had tried to kill another police officer in California. He had been on a crime spree the week that the Dallas police officer was killed, even though he was 16 years old. Then, of course, I *met* David Harris and started following him around. And he had just been paroled from prison. He had been in prison in California; he'd just been paroled to his parents in Vidor, Texas. And we met, and we continued to meet. Then I was scheduled to film him, and he didn't show up for his appointment to be filmed! He had disappeared, and within the week he turned up in Jefferson County Jail in Beaumont, Texas, indicted for the murder of Mark Walter Mays, and was subsequently convicted of capital murder and sentenced to death. He was actually executed earlier this year.

How was your investigation conducted? Was this a team of people you were working with? Or was it you in your apartment, going through files?

It was principally me, interviewing people, going through files, doing research of one kind or another.

Each night, you're weighing the evidence of your suspects?

Yes. When the material accumulated, I [was considering the likelihood of] two stories going on at once. One is a story about inculpatory evidence and another is a story about exculpatory evidence. You're looking at two things, if you like, at the same time. You're looking for evidence that shows you that Randall Adams did it, or that David Harris did it, and you're looking for evidence that Adams didn't do it, or David Harris didn't do it. And as I went through the case, slowly but surely, the mountain of evidence connecting David Harris with the murder grew and grew and grew, and the evidence connecting Randall Adams with the murder just continued to shrink. Until there was scarcely any left.

> *"I could see the frame but I couldn't see the picture, and that was true of the transcript."*

Tell me about the impact *The Thin Blue Line* had on the case, and the aftermath once the film was released.

Well, it had impact in one very definite sense: Material from the film— actually several interviews from the film—were submitted as evidence in federal and state court. Material in those interviews actually showed that the major witnesses against Randall Adams committed perjury, one by one by one. So eventually the conviction was overturned, and Adams walked. And [later] I would hear stories about how the Dallas district attorney's office was going to retry him for the murder, but of course that was just, in my view, idle boasting, because they had no case. The case was gone. There's no way to retry him because the case that they had made had evaporated.

Were you responding to the verité approach with *Gates of Heaven* as well?

Yes. *Gates of Heaven* was very much a reaction to verité. In fact, we used to joke while we were making it that we'll take all the principles of verité and stand them on their head. Instead of a handheld camera, I'll make sure the camera's always on a tripod! And instead of observing people, and being as unobtrusive as possible, I'll have people talk directly to the camera, I'll have them look directly at the camera, and be as obtrusive as possible! Instead of lightweight equipment I'll use heavy equipment! Instead of not staging anything, I'll stage everything!

I assume you're going to throw out sync sound, too?

No, there's still sync sound there. It's also what the people say, the language that they use. They use real language. It's not been scripted by me. *That's* the documentary element. And it shows, I think, in one very powerful way that you can tell a documentary story completely differently than in the verité idea, and produce some very, very interesting and powerful real stuff in the process.

Why did you feel the need to create a new aesthetic that was purposefully responding to the principles or claims of verité?

The claim annoys me. The claim seems to me clearly false. Self-evidently false. Style is not *truth*. Just because you pick a certain style does not mean that you somehow have solved the Cartesian riddle of what's out there, that you no longer have to think about anything. You just adopt a methodology. It's almost like thinking that because *The New York Times* uses a certain font, that guarantees the truthfulness of every sentence written in the newspaper. That's total nonsense.

The Fog of War

What about your approach makes your films innovative?

I suppose I like to think of what I do as an essay on the *idea* of nonfiction.

How so?

I think of my most recent film, *The Fog of War*. I was at a press conference at the New York Film Festival and a journalist asked, "Are you aware you only interviewed one person?" And I said, "Yes, I am." It was a stylistic choice! Of course, one could easily imagine a film about Robert McNamara that took on a completely different character than *The Fog of War*. A documentary where you would have had an array of experts, or people who had been connected with McNamara in one way or another all commenting on the man … as well as hearing from McNamara himself. And, of course, I did none of that. I specifically *chose* to do none of that. I mean, there's a reason for it, but the minute you decide to do something that is different you put yourself in peril.

What do you mean by that—what kind of peril do you put yourself in?

It may be very difficult to put together.

In *The Fog of War*, audio recordings capture Lyndon Johnson and Robert McNamara discussing the escalating pressure of decisions regarding America's presence in Vietnam.

Photos courtesy of The McNamara Project, Inc.

In this creative graphic sequence from *The Fog of War*, numbers fall from the sky illustrating the firebombing of Japan.

Photos courtesy of The McNamara Project Inc.

Why, then, do you choose such an unusual approach to your subject matter?

I suppose breaking the rules of something—*that* interests me, just for its own sake, breaking certain kinds of narrative rules.

Beyond your choice of exclusively interviewing McNamara, what rules did you break in *The Fog of War*?

If I look at *The Fog of War* and things that I'm most proud about in the movie, I love the falling numbers over Japan, the whole sequence of the firebombing of Japan. And McNamara is telling you a very, very, *very* powerful story, a very important story. But I like to think that it's been communicated visually. The voice-over, the visuals combine in a way that a story is told. History can easily become overburdened by details. And so, in telling history, you have to chart a course through a morass of material. You have to tell a story, and you have to communicate the story powerfully.

You've chosen an innovative style, but there's also a lot of new information about the war and McNamara's choices that come out during the film. What most surprised you during the making of it?

I know, myself, when I started work on *The Fog of War*, I was not aware of the extent of the devastation of Japan by Allied bombing—67 cities. I'd heard of the firebombing of Tokyo, but did I know this continued week after week after week, and that Japan was virtually leveled even before we dropped the two atomic weapons? This was something that was new information, new history, and I wanted to find a way to powerfully present it in the movie, and I hope I succeeded.

Can you explain why Robert McNamara was so important to you? Why did he need to be the predominant character for you to tell that story?

He's important to an entire generation of people! In my generation, the generation that came of age during the Vietnam War, McNamara was a central figure; a reviled figure for many, many, many, many people. And when I started reading about him again, in the 1990s, he had just published his book *In Retrospect* in '95, and then two subsequent to that, it brought up all of these old memories, if you like, of the '60s. But it also made me realize that this man has been powerfully part of history. If you were trying to make a movie about the 20th century in some oddball fashion, but still nevertheless trying to grab ahold of the 20th century, you could do no better than to create a profile of this man.

When did you meet him?

The day we started filming. He came up for an interview, and I met him, and we started the interview. So it happened all at once—actually, before 9/11. It was in 2001 that I first met him.

Fast, Cheap & Out of Control interweaves conversations with a topiary gardener, a robot designer, a lion tamer, and an expert on naked mole rats in a funny and provocative meditation on creativity and obsession.

Photo courtesy of Fourth Floor Productions.

Why did you want to make *Fast, Cheap & Out of Control*?

Well, first of all I liked the idea that you could take four stories, seemingly unrelated stories, and weave them together into one narrative. And I liked the movie having a dreamlike quality. Most documentaries—not all of them, certainly, but most of them—are about some external reality. I suppose the very term *documentary* makes you think that is what documentary should be about, providing a description of an exterior world, a public world, a world that's available to all of us. But I don't think it has to be the case. Quite clearly, I don't think it has to be the case. But part of what documentary can be is subjective, an attempt to explore how people see the world, their own mental landscape, their own private way of seeing themselves and the world around them.

And conducting interviews with eccentric characters was the best way for you to explore their mental landscape?

I am a great believer that people, through how they speak, how they use language, reveal an enormous amount about who they are.

What was revealing about the characters in *Fast, Cheap & Out of Control*? How did you decide to cast that film? How did you meet them?

I called them on the phone. [Robot designer] Rodney Brooks lives right around the corner from me. I live in Cambridge, Massachusetts; he teaches at MIT. The gardener was just south of Boston, in Rhode Island. The lion tamer I had filmed years ago for the first time in connection with the film I wanted to make about Dr. James Grigson on violence. And I thought the lion tamer was an interesting way of looking at that phenomenon, the prediction of violence, or the control of violence. So I guess the last was the mole rat guy, Ray Mendez. I read about him in

The New York Times. I first read about the mole rats and then I talked to a number of scientists, who didn't really inspire me very much one way or the other. And I finally stumbled on Ray Mendez, who at that time was living in New York City. And I went and met him, and I liked him. And so there you go!

What were the obvious connections, for you, between these characters? I can imagine another filmmaker saying, these are four fascinating characters and I'm going to make four separate, short films about them. But did you conceive of this as an integrated story from the beginning?

Yes. From the very, very beginning I was going to call it—because I liked the title of Rodney's paper *Fast, Cheap & Out of Control*. That was going to be the name of the film. And it was always imagined that it was going to involve these four stories woven together. In practice that proved extremely difficult to pull off.

In the editing?

Yes. Someone once asked me about the editorial strategy in that movie, and it took literally *years* to edit and, at one point I gave up on it, completely, because I just could *not* edit it!

After years of struggling with it, can you describe the final structuring principle that allowed you to finish the film?

The principal was that there's a preamble, where you're really told that the movie is going to be crazy, and that it's going to mix really diverse things, just so you know what you're getting into at the outset. And then the four characters were laid out so you know, at least, you have orientation. It's like a primer on the four characters. There's Character A, Character B, Character C, Character D.

"It's a narrative free fall for the viewers, hopefully."

And then you bring the characters back, you shuffle the order, you keep shuffling the order, and then you start blending the stories. So that, for example, the narration of one character goes with the visuals of another. And then, two-thirds of the way through the movie, I like to think that you're in some kind of free fall; you're in some kind of strange land where it's a mixture of everything. So it's a narrative free fall for the viewers, hopefully.

You shot it and used material that was shot on many different formats?

There was video, there was Super 8, there was 16mm, there was Super 16mm, there was 35mm. It was reprocessed 35, as I described it, where we would film material off of television sets and then that was edited into the movie.

Can you describe how you went about blending the four characters' stories? Was there someone who was thematically categorizing these moments as you went along, putting these into bins? How was that managed, logistically?

It's a movie that could not have been made without an Avid, I can tell you that much. It was the first movie that I made with an Avid. There was media all over the place.

Given that you had media coming from so many diverse sources, the Avid nonlinear editing system made it possible to even to consider editing it. But there are a lot of elements in it: Karen Schmeer's editing, Bob Richardson's photography, Caleb Sampson's music. Were those collaborations taking place during the editing phase? In other words, were you making requests from the edit room? Were you asking, now we need this kind of shot?

No. You shoot a film and then you edit it. I mean, this thing was shot in the course of ten days, and then it was years and years and *years* putting it together.

Music is a powerful element in that film. Was the score something that you started working on during postproduction, or did you have a preconceived—

No, that started very late. I went through all kinds of attempts to make music work with it, and it was Caleb Sampson who really solved the problem. He created a really magnificent score for the movie.

Talk to me about the music in your films, more generally. How do you see music as a driving component of your rule-breaking narrative style?

It's essential. Properly considered, it's part of the narrative. It is an essential part of the narrative in every single film where I've used music extensively, which is every film after *Gates of Heaven* and *Vernon, Florida*. Music was totally essential in *The Fog of War*, essential in *The Thin Blue Line*—really essential in everything.

Why is music essential to your style?

Because it's yet another way of taking you outside of the real world and into some kind of dreamscape.

Innovative Editing: An Organic Process

Do you get very involved in the editing process?

Of course I do! I believe, in general, that directors who don't edit really aren't directors at all.

Tell me about *Fast, Cheap & Out of Control*. I know that you wanted to draw connections between four different people with very unusual occupations:. But the result was a juxtaposition of their perceptions and philosophies interwoven with musical portraits of their work. Perhaps you can tell me about how the editing process took place.

Well, *Fast, Cheap & Out of Control* was almost an editorial nightmare. I don't know if there's any movie quite like it. Although I know people have tried to imitate it subsequent to its release. But there are reasons why there are very few movies of that sort. They're impossible, *impossible* to edit. Juggling four stories at the same time and trying to make something that works for an audience.

You're considering the audience constantly while you're editing.

Yes. Because, of course, the presumption with every single film that I've made is that it's going to be in theaters. And, given that fact, it's essential that it works for people who are actually paying money to see it, actually going to see it in a theater. So it took me *years* to edit that film. And, as I said, I gave up on it at one point. I thought it was uneditable.

Why was that?

I think that the editorial process, at least in my films, becomes difficult, because I've been trying to reinvent at least some aspect of what I do in every film I've made. And so it's not really clear what kind of principal to use. *Gates of Heaven* was incredibly difficult to edit. And a whole number of very experienced editors looked at the footage and said, "I have no idea what to do with this. It's not clear to me that this is even *editable*."

Can you explain why that was their reaction?

Because there is really nothing quite like it. There's no model to fall back on. There's no other film that I know of that looks like *Gates of Heaven*, or operates like *Gates of Heaven*.

Can you be more specific? An editor who has experience cutting documentaries, who has seen a whole variety of interviews and archival material, who has worked with a wide variety of directors, with different ideas and approaches, why did your material leave such editors so confused? What's so innovative about your material that they didn't know what to do with it?

You said it in your question. If the process is not straight ahead, if it's not easy to identify, if it's something you're actually uncovering in editing, if it's emergent—if you like—in the editing, then it's a much, much more difficult thing to grab ahold of. You're actually creating something new!

But you seem to prefer an organic process, rather than structuring your ideas ahead of time.

I'm very suspicious of documentaries that you can describe with a topic sentence. I think that almost everything that I've done has been avoidance of that sort of thing. There are not movies that are "about *x*." Defined and circumscribed. And I think that in itself makes it very, very different.

Also, there are various techniques that people use to put together nonfiction. Whether it's narration of one form or another, and particularly voice-over narration, or various people commenting back and forth, a kind of attempted balance where people quite specifically give you two sides of the question, or provide perspective on an issue. These are all very, very familiar in documentary films. And to a very large extent I've avoided all of that in my films.

> *"I've been trying to reinvent at least some aspect of what I do in every film I've made."*

Why have you avoided traditional techniques?

Doesn't interest me. It's not so complicated. One of the things that's interesting about documentary is that you have an opportunity to *create* something, not just in terms of content but that's also stylistically, very different. And not just different from feature films, but different from other documentaries as well. It's the opportunity of doing something that is innovative. And I have played around in different ways with what it *means* to make documentaries.

How did you gain access to those people in a moment where everybody was obviously frozen?

I gained access because I was working essentially for the corporate client itself, and it became a priority to find people, to bring them in, and to put them on film. Our casting people handled it.

"It was unusually powerful advertising, but it was real."

The filming happened that week?

It happened very, very quickly. We had already cast a lot of people, real people, but they were going to be reciting written copy. They were going to be given lines that they were going to speak, and that really got thrown out and we went to people just simply being interviewed, with the Interrotron, in a studio. And it was unusually powerful advertising, but it was real.

The United Airlines campaign led you to secure other commercial work?

Yes. The producer of the Academy Awards in 2002 was Laura Ziskin. And Laura Ziskin saw the United Airlines spots and hired me to do that movie that opens the Academy Awards. And that's also on my Web site. It has, among other people, Gorbachev, Laura Bush, Iggy Pop, Walter Cronkite.

Steve Jobs, who was in the audience that year at the Academy Awards, saw my film. He liked the white background, he liked the style, and said, "Let's get that guy." And that was why I was hired by Apple. It's as simple as that. And away we went, and filmed hundreds of people for Apple. Not all of them got on the air, but there were a lot of really, really great ones.

Do you have a favorite?

I probably do have a favorite, and it's probably the one I did with my son, Hamilton. And it's one that Steve Jobs really, really liked without even knowing

that it was my son, and it ran nationally, and there were 10-foot-high moving pictures of my son in the front of various Apple stores.

What appeals to you about that one?

Well, because I did a good job, with someone who I love. And he really comes across well. He's funny, he's charming. And it's just a damn good commercial. I have to agree with Mr. Jobs here, it's a good commercial even independent of the fact that he's a close personal relative!

The United Airlines campaign led to the Academy Awards film which led to the Apple "Switch" commercials. Did those help to reestablish your commercial reputation as someone who directs *real* people as well as actors?

Now, I do all kinds of things, from real people, to actors looking like real people, to real people looking like actors—and every permutation and combination in between. *Cross-pollination* would be the best way to describe it. A lot of the techniques I've learned in commercials I've applied to my documentary filmmaking and vice versa.

Can you give me an example of that cross-pollination? How do your documentary methods inform your spot work, and vice versa?

Well, the Interrotron is the clearest example in commercials, because I now use it quite often. Whenever you're asking real people to express themselves and to speak at length—regardless of how much material you use in the end, you want a stream-of-consciousness narration—Interrotron is always the best device for that sort of thing. So I try to avoid doing too many spots, too many commercials, that depend on the Interrotron. I like to use it less, rather than more. But people are now aware of it in the commercial business so, yes, I'm called upon to use it. I used it most recently with B.B. King. He advertises a diabetes measuring device. Of course, the most recent example of the Interrotron is this campaign that was done for the Democrats last summer. And there are about 50-plus spots that were shot for MoveOn.org.

From the Apple "Switch" campaign. "I probably do have a favorite, it's the one I did with my son, Hamilton. It's one that Steve Jobs really, really liked without even knowing that it was my son, and it ran nationally, and there were 10-foot-high moving pictures of my son in the front of various Apple stores."

Photos courtesy of Apple Computer.

It was the Democrats' own "Switch" campaign, of sorts.

Correct. People wrote, "Well, he's just imitating the Apple 'Switch' campaign." And then someone wrote in and said, "Well, he *did* the Apple 'Switch' campaign." And then someone else said, "And the Apple 'Switch' campaign was imitating the Academy Awards film, which he did previously," which is, in fact, the case. By and large—not that there aren't lots of historical antecedents to what I do—but it's been a lot of imitating myself.

"You are trying to create a kind of mental landscape, a fantasy world, a collection of ideas."

Do you have a standard process for approaching commercial work?

I'm not sure what you mean.

When you get a call like that, from Apple's agency, is it something where you start thinking, "OK, who have I met recently that would be right for this?" Or, "We should start casting sessions." Do you storyboard your spots? Do you start scripting? What is your reaction to a new, interested prospective client?

To me, whether it's a feature-length film or it's a 30-second commercial, you are trying to create a kind of mental landscape, a fantasy world, a collection of ideas. And advertising in this respect is no different than much longer films. I try to think about it in terms of the brand, what people are trying to *say*, what needs to be communicated. I think about it conceptually. I like to think that one of the things I do well is, I find ways of visually presenting information that are striking. That I'm able to take a complex idea and express it in visual form in a way that is elegant, simple, and powerful. It's hard talking about yourself this way, but I do think it's one of the things I'm good at.

D A **Pennebaker**

Chris **Hegedus**

Directors

Capturing Character

D A (DONN ALAN) PENNEBAKER

MOST FANS OF DOCUMENTARY KNOW D A PENNEBAKER'S FILMS. He is one of the most prolific pioneers of cinema verité filmmaking working today. But it may be surprising to learn what drove him to achieve this pioneer status: a personal "frustration" with the creative limitations of bulky filmmaking gear, where capturing real-life "theater" with sync sound was not possible. In 1953, Pennebaker made his first short film, *Daybreak Express*, and then proceeded to use his formal training and background as a mechanical engineer—combined with ingenuity and sheer determination—to invent both a style for nonfiction film and new film production equipment that made that style possible.

Pennebaker began in the 1950s by experimenting with existing film camera equipment, shooting mainly in New York. But when he went to shoot in Russia, he identified the need for a new kind of camera that would provide "a general solution … one camera that you could shoot on the stage at the Metropolitan Opera House, and you could take out to a desert and shoot. At that point," he explains, "nobody knew how to record sync sound in the field." So Pennebaker engaged in a mission to rebuild the cameras. He tapped his loose network of

D A Pennebaker filmography

Director

Elaine Stritch at Liberty (2004), with Chris Hegedus and Nick Doob

Only the Strong Survive (2002), with Chris Hegedus

Down from the Mountain (2002), with Chris Hegedus and Nick Doob

Searching for Jimi Hendrix (1999), with Chris Hegedus

Bessie: A Portrait of Bessie Schonberg (1998), with Chris Hegedus

Moon Over Broadway (1997), with Chris Hegedus

Victoria Williams: Happy Come Home (1997), with Chris Hegedus

The War Room (1993), with Chris Hegedus

Branford Marsalis: The Music Tells You (1992), with Chris Hegedus

Little Richard (1991), with Chris Hegedus

Comin' Home (1991), with Chris Hegedus

Jerry Lee Lewis (1990), with Chris Hegedus

▶ **For the past 30 years, Chris Hegedus and D A Pennebaker have collaborated on dozens of award-winning documentary films. "I think one of the things that's bonded us in our relationship," Hegedus says, "is we have a very similar vision of our films. I think if we thought artistically in totally different ways, we wouldn't be very compatible as filmmakers."**

Photos courtesy of Pennebaker Hegedus Films.

friends, at the same time he searched for technical solutions for everything from portable batteries to clocks that would synchronize sound to picture. Pennebaker spent years experimenting with fellow filmmakers Richard Leacock, Bob Drew, and Albert Maysles, until, in 1959, he became part of Drew Associates. As part of the Drew Associates team, Pennebaker helped create "the first fully portable 16mm synchronized camera and sound system," enabling events to be captured as they unfolded before the camera.

These technical achievements, however, are that much more impressive when put beside the innovations in filmmaking they enabled. Direct cinema—as defined by Pennebaker Hegedus Films—"…revolutionized the documentary genre by discarding narration, reenactments and other staged techniques in favor of direct and uninterrupted observation, creating a fly-on-the-wall sense of immediacy." Working with Drew Associates, Pennebaker made milestone films such as *Crisis, Primary*, and *Jane*. Along with Maysles Films, the Drew Associates creative team revolutionized both nonfiction cinema and American television journalism, creating the first cinema verité films in the United States.

In the early 1960s, Pennebaker moved on from Drew Associates to work with Richard (Ricky) Leacock, Shirley Clarke, and others, making character-driven, groundbreaking documentary films. In the 1960s, his unvarnished portrait of Bob Dylan, *Dont Look Back*, and the seminal *Monterey Pop* became "two of the earliest films using real-life drama to have a successful theatrical distribution."

In 1977, he partnered with director/producer Chris Hegedus to form Pennebaker Hegedus Films. Today, now married, they carry on the verité filmmaking tradition.

During Bill Clinton's first presidential race, they shadowed his campaign advisors James Carville and George Stephanopoulos to make *The War Room*, for which they received both the D.W. Griffith Award for Best Documentary of the Year and an Academy Award nomination. They recently codirected (with Nick Doob) a film for HBO, *Elaine Stritch at Liberty*, which was awarded three Primetime Emmy nominations including Outstanding Direction of a Music, Comedy, or Variety Program.

CHRIS HEGEDUS

Director Chris Hegedus came to filmmaking after being inspired (in art school) by the early direct cinema films of Bob Drew and D A Pennebaker. She didn't originally consider film as a career because, she says, "there weren't very many women role models in film when I was young. Then I saw *Primary* and *Jane*, and they really changed my life." Unlike much of the inaccessible experimental work being made at the time, Hegedus saw Drew and Pennebaker's films as "documentaries that weren't covered with narration telling me how to think. They followed real-life stories with character development and a dramatic arc just like fiction films. The films seemed so real because they were very contemporary, they were telling stories about my own time, and that really affected me." After coming to New York to pursue a career as an artist, she met up with Pennebaker and began editing his films.

"The nice part about going to see Penne was that he had a whole wall full of films that he had shot but had never edited. Our very first collaboration was *Town Bloody Hall*, which was about the women's movement and a now-infamous 1971 event with Norman Mailer moderating a panel that included Germaine Greer, the president of the National Organization for Women, and Jill Johnston, who was a wonderfully outrageous lesbian writer for the *Village Voice*. The audience was full of New York writers and intellectuals. Penne

Hegedus and Pennebaker hang out with the cast of *The War Room*, a film that followed Bill Clinton's 1992 Presidential campaign.

Photo courtesy of Pennebaker Hegedus Films.

had this wonderful event documented, and just sitting there. So I edited it for him. Then eventually, we started working together—shooting, editing, and directing films."

With *Town Bloody Hall,* Hegedus began a filmmaking partnership that has lasted for decades. "It was a very political time," she recalls. "At that time 16mm sync sound equipment really lent itself to making films about the moment. There was the Vietnam War, the women's movement; there was a lot of fervor and activity. And making very formalistic art films just seemed to be beside the point to me. You really wanted to be involved in the excitement of what was going on and this was the way to do it. So when I met Pennebaker I was overjoyed, because he had all this equipment."

Since their first codirecting collaboration in the mid-'70s, Hegedus has partnered with Pennebaker on a host of acclaimed films, including 1998's *Moon Over Broadway* (cited by *The New York Times* as the Best Documentary of the Year) and 1994's *The War Room*. In 2003, the team released *Only the Strong Survive,* "about some of the legends who made rhythm and blues music famous, including Isaac Hayes, Rufus and Carla Thomas, Wilson Pickett, and Sam Moore, among others." It premiered at the Cannes Film Festival and was distributed theatrically by Miramax Films.

Pennebaker Hegedus Films is one of the few production companies in the U.S. that actively produces feature-length documentaries each year, many of which are distributed theatrically. In 1989, they released the feature *Depeche Mode 101,* about the popular British synth-pop band. Pennebaker and Hegedus codirected *Elliot Carter at Buffalo,* about the American composer; *DeLorean,* a profile of the automobile entrepreneur John DeLorean; *Rockaby,* a document of the staging and performance of Samuel Beckett's play of the same name, and *Dance Black America,* a record of a four-day festival celebrating African American dance.

From the 1953 film *Daybreak Express,* D A Pennebaker's first documentary short. "I had made a 5-minute film. It wasn't my first—my first was *Baby,* a home movie about my 3-year-old daughter, Stacy—but it was a serious effort, which I used with the Duke Ellington record of the same name."

Photo courtesy of Pennebaker Hegedus Films.

▶ **Dont Look Back**, now in DVD, is still one of the company's highest grossing titles. Frazer Pennebaker, producer at Pennebaker Hegedus Films, explains, "When my father started filming **Dont Look Back**, Bob Dylan was not a big deal. [D A Pennebaker] took a crapshoot and it paid off. On **Dont Look Back**, we're 50/50 partners with Dylan. The film has done extremely well over the years."

Photo courtesy of Pennebaker Hegedus Films.

Can you describe what you were trying to achieve as a cameraman?

DAP: We needed a general solution. We needed one camera that you could shoot on the stage at the Metropolitan Opera House, and you could take out to a desert and shoot. At that point, nobody knew how to do sync. So we built five cameras, and they all worked, which was really miraculous, because they were all hand-made. We used those peculiar cameras into the '80s.

You produced *Jane* while you were part of Drew Associates?

DAP: Hope Ryden was my partner on that. She did the sound, and I filmed. We had other people working on it, but we did most of that film ourselves, just the two of us. It taught me that you didn't need a lot of people to make a feature. You just needed a good story, or Jane Fonda. You could make a film in any place where there was dramatic activity taking place, with characters that were interesting and believable. I went off with her for a month. We lived with her, because she wanted us to be there. She *wanted* the movie to be made. And that's almost always the case.

You find that when the subject is supportive of your presence the end result is more successful?

DAP: When we did *The War Room*, they wanted us there—even though they were frightened when we were there that Clinton would catch us. We'd come in after a week or so away, they'd say, "Oh, you should have been here." Whatever we missed would somehow come up, and they would reenact it. I don't know how they did it, but that's what always happens. So you know you can count on that. You don't have to set up an elaborate plan or a script, or tell people what to do. You don't have to direct anyone. In fact, the less directing you do, the more effective they'll be. It's the directing that kills it, because then they say, "Well, if that's what he wants, let's do it, and then we can get out of here." But when they're involved in putting it together, it's creative for them, too. It's just as interesting for them. More interesting.

A Conversation with Haskell Wexler

Directing Real-Life Characters

Cinematographer Haskell Wexler began shooting documentary films in the 1950s with his contemporaries D A Pennebaker, Ricky Leacock, and Albert and David Maysles. Today, working primarily on the West Coast, Wexler balances his dedication to social activism with an impressive career in Hollywood. Over the years, Wexler has worked with a number of highly regarded feature film directors, including Elia Kazan, Mike Nichols, Woody Allen, Milos Forman, George Lucas, and Francis Ford Coppola, on films such as *American Graffiti*, *In the Heat of the Night*, and *One Flew Over the Cuckoo's Nest*. He's received Academy Awards for his cinematography on *Who's Afraid of Virginia Woolf?* and *Bound for Glory*. In *Medium Cool,* a film he directed, Wexler shot on location at Chicago's 1968 Democratic Convention. He combined documentary and fiction footage in a blended approach that was controversial at the time.

You were instrumental in the development of cinema verité cinematography working with the Maysles brothers, D A Pennebaker, Robert Drew, and Ricky Leacock. How was your approach distinct from theirs?

HW: The big argument I always had with Al and David Maysles was they said, "Look, we're just recording what is; this is verité, this is the truth." And I would say, "Of course we coach people!"

For example, on *Salesman*, we were in a hotel room with all these Bible salesmen, and nothing was happening in the room, and they hired me on to be the second camera. I suggested to David that he call the wife of one of the Bible salesmen and tell her that we're here in Las Vegas with her husband in room so-and-so, and that he's having a good time. Just euphemistically. Then he hung up the phone, and he had a bug on the phone, and I was ready to shoot. Phone call comes, and the Bible salesman gets on the phone, and he says, "Well, no, Honey. Oh, yes, no. We're doing work. No, no, I haven't gone to any of those shows." And so we had a little scene. You know what I'm saying?

So you set it up a little bit, to stimulate natural drama.

HW: See, the thing is, Al and David always denied that they do it, but all of us in cinema verité filmmaking, we are not like the surveillance cameras in the supermarkets.

Al Maysles said, "It's not shooting like a fly on the wall because a fly doesn't have a brain." You're taking the next step by saying you want to provoke actions with your characters in a way that's going to make it a good film.

HW: Yes. My definition of *cinema verité* is to *use* your filmmaking ability. For example, I actually did that with an IMAX camera, shooting behind the scenes for the Rolling Stones IMAX. In the scene, Keith Richards walks into the shot and they start jamming and goofing around and so forth. Well, I knew for a scene that I needed a shot of Richards coming in the door so it would cut better. After I shot all this stuff I said, "Keith, would you mind coming in the hotel room door?" So then, bing! I turned the big mother camera on, and he comes in the door, walks out of frame.

Sounds innocent enough, but is that breaking the rules of direct cinema? You're no longer just presenting events as they unfold before the camera.

HW: All documentary filmmakers, in one way or another, by the very selection of what lens they use, what time of day they shoot, what people are in the shot, what remains in the film, and what remains out of the film, it's all a creative process, and it is not, as some purists used to maintain, just "recording reality." There is no "reality." Once images are recorded, by whatever medium, they cease to be reality. It becomes the filmmaker's reality. All the images we see are images now presented by the people who are able to present them. And they don't necessarily represent the truth.

When the president makes a speech, he's had directors tell him how to talk, he has script writers who put stuff on the TelePrompTer, he has answers to questions one, two, three, and four—which is not unique to the president. It's true whenever people go public. And this has to do with the subject that I'm very interested in.

When I was young they used to say, "Well, I have photographic *proof*!" That photograph, it captures that moment. And that meant verité—that means truth. Well, certainly, in filmmaking particularly, in motion picture filmmaking, we can alter things—in post or even in camera—to make them look diametrically different. I guarantee you, from having personal experiences, not only on features but in documentaries, that the sanctity of the visual image is in the control of the person who owns it, and not in anyone else's control.

As one of the pioneers of direct cinema, Pennebaker used his engineering background to invent lightweight, portable 16mm cameras with sync sound that allowed filmmakers to capture spontaneous events, people, and places without narration or reenactments. Here, he shoots Bo Diddley.

Photo courtesy of Pennebaker Hegedus Films.

Jimi Hendrix in *Jimi Plays Monterey*, one of several films the Pennebakers made about Hendrix.

Photo courtesy of Pennebaker Hegedus Films.

The Changing Definition of *Documentary*

How do you know when a verité film is finished?

DAP: You usually knew it was finished when you got bored. You didn't want to take any more pictures; you didn't want to be around the person you were filming. You wanted to go home and edit it. But now, that isn't the case because it's much more Proust than it was in the beginning. In the beginning it was Hemingway. Now [that we're shooting digitally] it's fallen into that marvelous floating thing of, "We'll go until it doesn't go."

What do you mean by that—it was once Hemingway and now it's "much more Proust"? Has your relationship to the film medium changed?

DAP: I used to write little short stories a la Hemingway. I had a teacher at Yale, my spelling was so bad he said, "If I correct your spelling you'll fail totally." But he said, "I will ignore your spelling if you'll write me a story every day." So I did. You start off, "It's a lonely road, the cars are coming." It has a beginning, maybe it's got some violence, and then it's got an ending. So, you look for that curve that provides the beginning and middle and an end. And that's your story. If you can do it in a day, great. If it takes a month, it takes a month. Those were the stories we did in early direct cinema.

Now, you go to the heart of a novel of good writing, *any* good writing, the reason it is good has nothing to do necessarily with how well it's written. But if it's *about* something, or somebody who knows something, and you want to know what they know, that's how you get it. You get it from the book. You can't get it by osmosis. You can't get it by footprints. You have to read what they thought about.

You're saying that documentaries today are cultural reference points through which people learn about one another's human experience, and ultimately better understand their own?

DAP: I think in ten years people are going to look back on this time and they're going to say, "In those days they used to have movies with people acting in them." It'll be a different sense of what propels a movie. It's character, and it's what characters *know*. And that's what Proust proved: You don't have to write it. The story doesn't have to keep bending, or have climaxes. The climaxes are *within* your life. That was a new idea, and it caught people's attention—everybody from Virginia Woolf to all kinds of writers who were digging up material. I think documentary film is responding to that idea. Narrative film doesn't.

Why do you think real stories are more entertaining than fiction, today?

DAP: Because all [fiction writers] could do is regenerate stories that are already done, but with new characters, with new celebrities. Well, after a while you get tired of *Captains Courageous* endlessly. You want something different. Because you know all that now. Everybody knows it.

CH: Reality shows are a kind of Proust.

DAP: Yes, that's true. I think that the process, if there is an art, it's that you can tell if it leads to some kind of distribution. The great painters are always in advance of their paintings. But it's a little hard on the artist, and it's hard on the filmmakers. But you do what you have to do; you can't always be guided by your agent.

Are there practical challenges with making documentaries today, when there are fewer boundaries, and the format is less constrained?

DAP: Yes. And we're still looking for how to deal with it. It's impossible! The film we're doing on Al Franken could go on for four more years because he's going to run for the Senate. Well, we can't wait four more years. We can hardly afford to shoot for another month, you know? And nobody wants to buy a film that's endless. They don't know what to do with it, either.

A Conversation with Sheila Nevins

The Changing Definition of *Documentary*

Time Warner's HBO/Cinemax is one of the largest production and acquisitions outlets for documentary programming in the United States. Sheila Nevins, the president of HBO Documentary and HBO Family, joined Home Box Office in 1979. Subscriber-based television was not well-established when she first learned about the job opening for her previous position at HBO, director of documentary programming. Nevins remembers, "I didn't even know what HBO was. I thought this job involved directing documentaries, and so I said I didn't know many directors. I said, "Let me look through my files." I then went to the 42nd Street library, and I read about Home Box Office. And I said, "This is a great thing! This is cable, and this is no commercials, and this is uninterrupted movies, maybe I should take this job." So I took the job thinking I was going to direct documentaries, and when I arrived at the job interview, I realized I was going to be the director *of* documentaries. And that's how I got the job. Serendipitously, accidentally, and on purpose, simultaneously."

Tell me about the first documentaries that you produced for HBO.

SN: I thought a documentary was like Winston Churchill, his boyhood and his rise to manhood. Hitler, the evil being. I didn't know anything, so I just did them. I went out and found people to make them.

You commissioned independent directors to produce for HBO?

SN: I'd just call them up and say, "You're not going to believe this, but I have this job now. I have to make 25 documentaries." And I would give out assignments, and they would give me a budget, and we would approve it, and make it. I would supervise it.

Today, HBO's documentaries dominate the best documentary category at most every major film festival and awards program. They're usually character-driven, often covering shocking topics in a contemporary style. How did your producing approach change over the years?

SN: Somewhere between Churchill and Hitler and World War II and the Depression, I realized that this was a movie channel, and maybe I shouldn't be making real

"You married me for my camera?!"

making very formalistic art films just seemed to be beside the point to me. So when I met Pennebaker, I was overjoyed, because he had all this equipment.

DAP: You married me for my camera?!

Ricky was in the process of getting a divorce and had to get out of town, and our company was about to liquidate itself. It was just on the edge of bankruptcy, and everybody had departed. So I was there alone with a stalwart friend who was minding the office for us, Edith van Slycke. We had no money or anything. We just had a lot of old films that we'd shot. And Chris walked in, and said she was looking for a job. So I said, "OK. We'll hire you." I remember Edith saying, "What will you hire her with? We don't have any *money*." I said, "We'll figure it out." I think Chris worked for very little money for a long time.

CH: That's still standard, I think.

Earlier, you both mentioned that one of the things that drew you to documentary was the fact that you could make a film by yourself. Yet you've worked together on dozens of films. What's so attractive to you about this partnership?

DAP: Even though I like the idea of making a film by myself, I like having a partner around to show it to. That's part of the impulse—you need to test yourself against somebody, and they have to be somebody that you think is your peer. I'd had partners before, but Ricky was the only person I'd ever thought of as beyond peer—Ricky was a father figure for me in some way, even though he probably would deny that now, I don't know. But that was what drew me to him in the beginning. When I did something, his reaction would be meaningful. I needed somebody who I thought knew more than I did.

Describe how the partnership developed.

CH: Once we started working together we got money to do a film that ended up taking two years of our lives. It began when the Corporation for Public Broadcasting announced that it had money to do a political series. We went down

From *Town Bloody Hall*, Hegedus's first collaboration with Pennebaker. Pennebaker says, "Chris knew a lot more about the women's movement than I was ever going to know. And I certainly did not want to make a film that would be a laugh at the expense of the women's movement."

Photo courtesy of Pennebaker Hegedus Films.

to Washington and talked to a man who was very involved with what was going on to find a political story to pitch.

DAP: It was based on a book, and a series of articles in a magazine.

CH: Richard Whalen was his name. He said, "You're not going to believe this, but the most important issue—this was during Jimmy Carter's administration—is the president's energy bill. But surprisingly, the biggest problem is not going to be oil. It's going to be a fight over natural gas in this country." And we went, "Natural gas? That sounds *really* boring." But he said, "No, believe me, this is going to be the big fight in Congress." So we started filming, and it ended up being one of the longest legislative battles ever in Congress, with a filibuster by amendment, which was eventually outlawed. In politics, the economy, and in Iraq it's still all about energy policy and much of it can be traced back to that bill.

How did you go about shooting *Energy War* in Washington, D.C., during such a heated time?

D A Pennebaker and Albert Maysles speak to an audience of filmmakers about their experiences developing direct cinema.

Photo courtesy of Pennebaker Hegedus Films.

CH: We followed all sides of the issue, from the Administration and its lobbyists, to the natural gas producers, to the congressmen and senators who were fighting for or against the bill. And we had all sorts of filmmakers working with us. We collaborated with Pat Powell on this film, and we hired—as very young filmmakers—Ross McElwee and Michel Negroponte. Nick Doob, our partner here, worked on it as well. And Joel DeMott and Jeff Kreines are wonderful filmmakers who filmed with the natural gas producers in Texas. So we had this group of filmmakers all following different aspects of the story simultaneously.

DAP: Who didn't talk to each other except at night, secretly. Because if the Administration found you were talking to the other side, we didn't know what would happen. They really were very smart. The politicians knew a lot of what was going on, which we didn't. That was their business, to know what was going down. And we assumed, because we were somewhat secretive and hung out in restaurants, and talked at night on the telephone, that people wouldn't know.

That wasn't the case? You and your crew descended on Washington in the late '70s, and it was not a clandestine project?

DAP: Well, I'm sure that everyone there knew *exactly* what we were up to! But they tolerated us, because we seemed too ineffective. For instance, you weren't supposed to film in the hall of the Senate outside of the various offices—in these beautiful floor-tiled hallways and whatnot, where everybody would come out and talk to each other. So we thought, that's a great place to film, and we went up there and filmed people who would talk to us or talk to each other. We were always on the edge of the law. And of course, you weren't allowed to film in the Senate, and you weren't allowed to film in the House.

The film traced a battle over a bill in Congress, but you weren't allowed to *film* in Congress? How did you capture what was going on?

DAP: They had these TV systems, so the various members of the House could see what was going on from their offices. We got one of the ones we knew, a guy from Rhode Island, to let us into his office, and we'd go in at night and film off the screen.

CH: This was before C-SPAN, when debates in the House and Senate were not on television. *The Energy War* has some amazing characters in it. It has a very, very young Al Gore in it. And Gary Hart. A lot of people who've gone on to have careers in politics that have spanned the decades.

DAP: It's a fascinating film. We're just now redoing it, because it's five hours long. In the beginning, James Schlesinger took a very dim view of us. In fact, the first day we went to see him—we were going to show him a film or talk to him. He had an office in the basement of the White House. They said, "You can't see him until after lunch." So we went in to a movie and suddenly, in the middle of the movie, this voice over the PA system said, "Pennebaker, come to the White House." I couldn't believe it! They knew where we were. We went in, and Schlesinger looked at us and said, "I know who you are. You're snoops, and I don't want you anywhere around me or anything we're doing." I said, "Oh, well, that's too bad." We were summarily dismissed. And by the end of that film—this is amazing—he was taking us around in his limo to make sure we got to places we needed to be to get the story right.

Why did Schlesinger change his tune about supporting you over the course of the film?

DAP: Because he saw that we were seriously trying, that we weren't dealing in whatever the double dealings were of Washington—he saw that we were really trying to get the history, and that knocked him out. And, in fact, he got us into the coatroom of the Senate, where we could hear the vote on the PA system, and we could record it. And he knew we were doing it. We were getting stuff that nobody else was getting in the news media, just because he would help us. Schlesinger was terrific.

Describe his role in the political drama, and why your sincerity moved him.

DAP: He was a Republican who, for some reason, Carter hired to try to get the old boy network to function. And he would admit it, you know? He would look up and laugh in the middle of a phone call and say, "The old boy network." But he was so earnest about what he thought had to be done. He really looked on us as a part of his operation.

Shooting Verité, Developing Character

All of your films feature memorable characters. Some, like Bob Dylan, were not all that famous when you began filming them, but would become very well known. Others, like Kaleil Isaza Tuzman and Tom Herman from *Startup.com*, were everyday citizens. Your approach to shooting these characters creates an unusual sense of intimacy with them. In the beginning of a film, you're less concerned with capturing the action or recording the sound than developing a familiarity with the person's image for the audience.

DAP: Then, as it gets going, Chris is out there with a wireless mic or a boom mic close to the subject, and you can't hear; you're too far away because you're taking a portrait. You do it from the vantage of being outside of the area. You start moving in. At one point, about halfway through the films, I used to take off the zoom and put on a small wide-angle lens. It was so wide that I could just point the camera. I didn't even have to look through a finder.

How was that advantageous, to shoot constantly with a wide-angle lens?

DAP: I could put it on my shoulder and have eye contact with people. I could join groups and hear what they were saying, and know that I was getting it. The wide-angle lens became the finishing lens for a film. It's where the filmmaker *joins* all the people he's filming, and becomes one of them.

[continued on page 104]

◀ **David Bowie in *Ziggy Stardust*, and John F. Kennedy in *Primary*. Pennebaker: "In the beginning you're pretty much at the end of your telephoto, and you're getting portraits of people just the way you would if you were taking stills. This filming goes back to the way people behaved thousands of years ago. Two families would meet, they could hardly talk to each other because they didn't share the same language. They had to find ways of transmitting information and ideas. It came by concentrating, they had to *look* very hard, they had to try to understand body language, and all sorts of things that we've thrown away now."**

Photos courtesy of Pennebaker Hegedus Films.

Thinking Behind the Camera

DAP [*to Chris*]: I've never asked you this before but I've been asked this myself: When you're filming, and it's something hard, are you thinking about it? What's going on in your head when you're filming?

CH: No, I'm totally absorbed in the moment. It's very concentrated but I'm just looking.

DAP: Are you thinking of the shot in terms of how to cut the scene? Are you thinking of it as an editor?

CH: All those things flash into one's mind when filming. How am I going to use this? Do I need other shots? That's why people who actually shoot film or record the sound often understand what you need to make the story in the editing room.

DAP: It's like a tune going through your head. It's totally engaging. I find I'm not thinking much at all. Although I think I should be thinking more. But I'm depending on you to be thinking more. I'm really like a person swimming: I'm just in the water and I have no particular direction or anything, but I know that I'm in the water and that what I'm going to have to do is deal with the water.

MC: In *Dont Look Back*, there's a scene where Dylan and Joan Baez are singing together. You chose an unusual way to shoot them, playing with focus and zoom throughout the scene. It's poetic. What were you reacting to?

DAP: I have no idea. At any time, if you interrupted me when I'm filming and said, "What's on your mind?" I would feel very foolish, because I have nothing on my mind. It would be like you discovered me looking out the window, like a cat. I would have nothing on my mind at all.

CH: A lot of the times shots are framed a particular way just out of practicality. After the film is done somebody could look at a frame and deconstruct it and say, "Oh, he did this and that" but, really, it was shot that way because that was the only spot you could be in to get the shot. As a cameraperson, you try to be in the most interesting, best spot you can, or, you're where you are because you don't want to move and interrupt the situation. That's a lot of what we're doing—we're not trying to be flies on the wall, we want life to go on so that we can film it and record it in some way. And if you're always moving all around the room to get the right picture of a shoe tapping or something, because you think that's arty, chances are they may not want you there, and you are disrupting what's going on; you just make such a nuisance of yourself. There are all different reasons the film is framed or shot in a certain way, especially in our type of movie.

DAP: The camera is most effective as the gathering instrument, the witnessing instrument, when the person guiding it is looking at it the same way you look out a train window—with no other impulses. It's like meditation, where you clear your mind so you can have the greater consciousness enter. I could never imagine how you could do that, except when I look through a camera I know that I do it without meaning to or wanting to.

There's another aspect: the difference between the scripted camera and what I consider to be the "looking out the window" camera.

How is that shooting style different?

DAP: When you go to the theater, the audience is watching the scene take place on a stage. They're able to look at different parts of the scene as they wish. That is, the scene doesn't focus your attention. Good actors may focus attention on themselves when they say the lines, but some people don't want to follow that actor. So you get different people looking at different things on that stage. And when you're shooting a scene in a feature film, the camera is as scripted as any of the actors are. It looks at this thing close up, then there's a cutaway here; it's all scripted. Reality isn't like that. You don't sit in your room looking at things that way. But you accept it in scripted films, because that's the way it's done, and has always been. In a documentary, when you take the unscripted camera, and you look at a scene going on, you realize the camera can look anywhere it wants, that the camera doesn't have a script to follow, and it gives it a sense of possibility that you're never going to get from a narrative film. Never.

Because the specific actions captured in a cinema verité documentary shoot cannot be predicted, you're making creative choices spontaneously in the field.

DAP: I think one of the interesting things in *Dont Look Back* is, in the beginning you have a problem that dramatists have. Which is, you've got an empty stage and you've got to put some people on it that the audience is going to recognize, or know why they're there.

In feature films, you recognize Clark Gable, you know him the minute he walks in the room. Nobody has to tell you when he later becomes some character in the story. But in a documentary, you have a whole lot of people that we've never seen before. And they don't come up in a nice order; they don't perform for you nicely. That's why it's important for the cinematographer to help identify your main character early on in the filming, by shooting portraits, close up.

Carol Burnett in *Moon Over Broadway,* a film about the making of a Ken Ludwig's star-crossed Broadway play.

Photo courtesy of Pennebaker Hegedus Films.

He was unhappy with your portrayal of him?

CH: He looked at it and said, "You know, I look like a real jerk in this." His wife, I remember, was watching it with him at the time, and she was so nice. I thought she was going to say something horrible, like, "You can't have this film be released." And instead she said, "No, Ken, you look like *yourself* in it." And what he realized in the process—and I thought this was so brave of him—he said, "I do come out badly in this. But this is the first film I've seen that really shows what it's like to produce a Broadway play. I don't think anybody else has done that before. Because of that, and because of my love for the theater"—a lot of his work is about the theater—he said, "put it out there." And he let it go. Those are the times where it's hard. Because you don't want to cause somebody pain.

DAP: That's it. In my mind, the guiding instinct that I have throughout a film is to "do no harm" to anybody, which is probably why I like the idea of just looking out the window, because you're not doing any harm when you're looking out a window. You can look at scenes that are filled with intertwining, adversarial motives, and you try to see them in a way that will do the least harm to anyone that you've gotten to like. I remember the thing in *The Energy War*, a guy who was working in [Senator Edward] Kennedy's office got very smart-assed and made some dumb statements. The guy said, when he saw it, "I'll be fired if you run that that way." At the time, I believed him. He was a very nice guy. We knew him and liked him. And I thought, "Jesus, no film is worth getting anybody fired. I don't care how involved you are in it."

You changed the film so he would not be fired?

DAP: Yes. We made a change, and when PBS found we'd made a change, they had a fit. They said you've got to write some disclaimer, which destroyed the entire scene. Actually, if I'd kept my mouth shut, we could've made it work so that he didn't say it. We could have done it. It wasn't even an important thing. But for some reason, I was just spouting off to the PBS person that was involved. And they took it as somehow that their whole palace would fall if it was thought that something had been changed at the request of the subject. I said, "Come on, the guy, he's just working, you know? He's not the president or the senator. Jesus, you don't want to screw him up like that." That's ridiculous, when it's just a little thing. I remember I thought afterwards, that teaches me to keep my mouth shut, because all those things are fixable. And you don't want to do harm to anybody, if you can help it. The idea of ruining somebody's life with a film seems horrifying to me.

Accessing Real-Life Drama

Making verité political films is different from interview- or research-driven documentaries. You're covering the story as it's unfolding before the camera. Many filmmakers find it challenging to collaborate on verité projects because there's such spontaneity; it's more difficult to plan out responsibilities. It's not like delegating where one person does research and another conducts interviews. How does your verité filmmaking approach affect your collaboration?

CH: We are both camerapersons, so we can do either role. In *The War Room* I took sound and Penne shot. During the filming part of making a movie you can feel very unloved because quite often the character doesn't necessarily want to have you there. They do when things are going well, but not when things become difficult. So I think having a partner is comforting, you become bonded together going through that struggle of not knowing where your story is going, especially on a long story like *The War Room*. It's really great to have somebody to go through the journey and adventure with. I think a lot of documentary filmmakers have partners, and do it with people.

DAP: Marry their sound person or marry their cameraperson.

CH: Some do get married. I think there are probably plenty of couples out there. Al Maysles partnered with his brother, David; Joan Churchill and Nick Broomfield worked together for quite a long time; Alan and Susan Raymond. There are a lot of documentary filmmakers that tend to pair up as friends or whatever, to go through the process, because it *is* a collaborative process. And it is nice to have somebody by you when you're going through this process, which quite often is a lonely one.

When you first started, one of you did sound, and one operated the camera?

CH: We did both.

An even division of labor.

CH: An even division of labor.

> *"His input is always very important to me, even when we disagree."*

Many filmmakers partner with another producer or director on one film, but your collaboration has spanned decades. What makes it work? Can you describe the dynamics of your collaboration?

CH: One of the things that has bonded us in our relationship is we have a very similar vision of our films. I think if we thought artistically in totally different ways, we wouldn't be very compatible as filmmakers. In terms of the division of roles, when I was working as a soundperson with Penne shooting, it was interesting, because often I would understand the story and what to film more than he would because I was closer.

Why is that?

CH: Because the stories are very dialogue driven. If you're listening to people, and what they're saying, then you're concentrating on *that*. And if you use radio microphones, you can hear what's going on. And sometimes you understand the details of the story or where it's going even more than the cameraperson does because a lot of times they tend to be further away and filming with zoom lenses.

We always collaborated on the filmmaking, because sometimes I have more of the story arc in my memory from having listened to it more than Penne has—and he could visualize it, because he knew what he shot. But our collaboration also worked because we have similar views. In the same way that access to your characters and story has to do a lot with respect for the people that you're filming, and what they're doing in their lives, and the privilege of being let into their lives, what makes a good collaboration between filmmakers is respect for their work and their abilities. Because I admired the films that Penne shot before we became partners, and I respect his opinions, I think that we have had a wonderful collaboration. His input is always very important to me, even when we disagree.

When do you disagree?

CH: That mostly comes in the editing.

Why is that?

CH: Because the editing is much more of an artistic part of the process. The making of the film is really following what's going on in the story, and filming it and *getting* it. It's a lot more process. The editing is much more creative and forming a story. Because of that, you have your individual personalities. You know, during every film we usually do get divorced once!

But the great thing about Penne is that he is very easy to give up his idea and see the other person's idea in a really fair way, which is hard to do.

[To Penne] I think it's harder for me than it is for you to do that. If I see something, I tend to want it that way. And luckily, you step aside and bear with me a lot of times—which is really nice.

Lauren Lazin

Director

Making Television
With a Conscience

L AUREN LAZIN IS NOT YOUR TYPICAL TELEVISION EXECUTIVE. SHE
recognizes the value of her show's strong ratings and the
importance of the MTV News and Specials department (which she
formed in 1992) to the network's public image. Her priorities,
however, are more closely aligned with an activist's or an independent
filmmaker's. Lazin remains committed to producing work that addresses social
issues affecting contemporary youth, and she's interested in working with the
film world's leading documentary filmmakers. As an executive who produces
dozens of shows a year, she's focused first on treating her show's real-life
characters with respect, and second with impacting viewers in a meaningful
way that touches their lives. "I tell filmmakers who come to us, 'Take everything
you *think* is MTV and just put that away, because that's not what we do here.'"

Prior to joining MTV, Lazin graduated from the acclaimed masters program in
Documentary Film Production at Stanford University. She came to New York in

from girls, all kinds of great things." The film is artfully timed to an impeccable score of Shakur's own rap music and relevant songs by others. In the tradition of MTV documentaries, many sequences correlated closely to the lyrics of popular songs. (At one point, amidst a creative montage of images of Shakur snuggling up sequentially with dozens of different female fans, the soundtrack turns to Sade's *Smooth Operator*.) Lazin's year-long research effort and diligent use of Shakur's archives paid off. In November 2003, *Tupac: Resurrection* opened theatrically on 800 screens through a distribution deal with MTV's sister company, Paramount Pictures, and was nominated for a 2005 Academy Award for Best Documentary.

• • •

From Music Videos to Meaty Stories

When you joined the network, it was still early in the evolution of cable television. What was MTV like?

I was part of the second wave of MTV. The first wave was videos and the second wave was actual programming. I was in a department called Special Programming. It included everything that wasn't a video, a promo, or a news piece; anything longer than three minutes was my area. We were considered "long-form programming."

Right away I started doing documentaries. Doug Herzog, who is now the president of Comedy Central—he's the man who hired me—actually told me the story that, the day he hired me, he turned to his assistant and said, "Can you imagine doing *documentaries* on MTV?"

But it worked out really well. I started off doing artist's biographies: Robbie Robertson, the B-52's, and Janet Jackson. And we did a few movie star biographies. Then, in 1990, I moved over to the news area, because I thought, that's where all the smart people were. I said, "Can we do documentaries that are *not* about celebrities? Can we do documentaries about something else? How about ideas and issues?"

▶ The B-52's, subject of one of the many rockumentaries Lazin produced and directed in her early days at MTV.

Photo by Janette Beckman, courtesy of Direct Management.

▼ A promotional card from *Sex in the '90s*, one of MTV's first non-celebrity-driven documentary series, which ran for a decade. Lazin says, "It was very light and fun and sexy, but it was also about parental consent for abortion, and homophobia in the music industry, and HIV testing. It was real stuff that really mattered."

Photo courtesy of MTV.

What was your first non-celebrity documentary at MTV?

The first one we did was on sex. It became a very long-running series called *Sex in the '90s*. It was very light and fun and sexy, but it was also about parental consent for abortion, homophobia in the music industry, and HIV testing. It was real stuff that really mattered. So, the ratings were great! The shows did well. And from there we branched out and did documentaries on drugs, on religious intolerance, and all kinds of interesting topics that affect young people.

Your department was separate from the MTV News group?

Yes.

What was the news group doing at the time?

They were doing their news reporting. They were covering artist stories, celebrity stories, and Artists Against Apartheid. Anything that happened in the news. Our department would expand it, and make longer documentaries about similar topics. But our division wasn't just celebrity-driven. My programming role models were people like Sheila Nevins at HBO and Pat Mitchell at Turner and people who had these really great documentary areas. I always thought, "Wouldn't it be great if we could do that here at MTV?"

Your goal was to expand the scope of the network's programming?

I wanted to produce programs that covered thought-provoking, interesting topics, but told in an MTV style.

For an audience unfamiliar with news and specials programming at MTV, can you talk about how MTV evolved from a music video channel to programming?

It evolved because the shows worked. And the more rigorous and thoughtful the pieces were, the higher the ratings were. At its cornerstone, it was because we trusted the audience. We believed our audience wanted to get really meaty, interesting stories. And we always were one of the highest-rated programs on the channel. Back when ratings for *Beavis and Butthead* were so high, our ratings were as high as *Beavis and Butthead*, and then they were as high as *The Real World*. And news and specials programs still do very, very well.

Beyond the ratings success, how does producing documentaries help achieve the goals of the MTV network?

They're certainly good for the channel in terms of image. In the beginning, they helped us not get kicked off of cable affiliates who were concerned about MTV's influence on young people. Because we'd be able to say, "Hey, we're also looking at guns and schools, and we're looking at other topics, and kids are watching it."

Urgent Programming, Impacting an Audience

In addition to on-air programming promotion, your department is very active with off-air outreach.

We've always made sure our documentaries include heavy educational outreach. We've even given our films to schools and libraries.

Why is that important?

One of the things I've always liked about doing documentaries on MTV is that the audience is really involved with the films. They're watching, they're attentive, and they interact. A lot of documentary filmmakers are motivated by outreach: They want to get their message out, they want to affect people. MTV has been a really direct way to do that.

> **news:docs** Presents *True Life: I'm Coming Out* from the award winning documentary series.

Can you give me an example of how MTV's documentaries affect the lives of your viewers?

About ten years ago, I directed a program on child sexual abuse called *Fight Back*— young people fighting back against child sex abuse. And we had an 800 number at the end of the piece where viewers could call for further information.

Every time that documentary ran they would get hundreds of phone calls from kids, hundreds and *hundreds* of phone calls. Eventually, we were then able to make the piece available for free from Blockbuster stores. And we heard from a lot of young people who took their abusers to court.

That's incredible.

Isn't it? I mean, there are people who took their abuser to court. And when they were asked, "What made you do this?" they said, "Well, I saw this documentary on MTV, and I learned how to do it." So our programming is a direct line to our target audience.

Does that happen often when you tackle social issues?

Yes. I executive-produced a documentary a couple years ago, *True Life: I'm Bipolar*, directed by Lucia Engstrom, on young people diagnosed as bipolar. And I can't begin to tell you how many requests we've gotten for that show from people who are friends of people who are bipolar, from parents who are asking, "What does

True Life: I'm Coming Out. **Still and promotional postcard. The *True Life* series tackled issues as serious as drug abuse, violence in schools, and teen pregnancy, all with the distinctive MTV look. "The *I'm Coming Out* episode had a huge effect on our viewers. Still, now, there will be gay kids who'll say, 'I saw that show, and that's what made me decide to come out. Because I saw someone else do it.'"**

Photo courtesy of MTV.

"I met all these great filmmakers—people who I really admired."

You seem to straddle the film and television worlds.

Traditionally, there's been a real divide between people who work in TV and people who make films. Filmmakers are very precious with their pieces, and they have to run on the festival circuit, and then maybe they'll come out on video or maybe they'll be on PBS. And I would say, thanks to people like [HBO Documentaries president] Sheila Nevins, who has broken down that divide, that's changing a little bit. At the Museum of TV and Radio, there's Television Curator Ron Simon, he's someone who really helped break down the divide. And Nancy Buirski, who runs the Full Frame Film Festival, that's one of the first documentary festivals that would show TV programs. It was great to see them on the big screen, and to have a dialogue. But, for years there were the films that were in festivals, and then there were films that were shown on TV. It was like two separate worlds.

It's surprising to me that you're not overwhelmed with pitch sessions and proposals. I would think that for documentary makers, it's nearly impossible to manage a career outside of television work. Is it financially possible to produce documentaries independently for film festivals in the hopes of securing theatrical distribution?

Well, when I first came to New York in the mid-'80s it was the tail end of the grant-making era, where you could actually write for grants for your film. I had directed a film, *The Flapper Story*, that was in festivals, and I met all these great filmmakers—people who I really admired, who were my heroes. When I spoke with them, they all would say, "I don't know how I'm going to send my kids to college. I don't know how I'm going to get money for my next documentary." And I thought, "You're the most famous person I know, who's made so many great documentaries! There's got to be a way, there's *got* to be a way."

Tupac: Resurrection

You're still working as a film director, though you're a television executive.

I've been making films all along. I didn't come here to just be an executive, I came here to be a documentary filmmaker, and I've always been able to make films while supervising other films and growing the department. Two years ago I took a leave of absence from my job at MTV to direct *Tupac: Resurrection*, which is a feature film for MTV Films, which then got picked up by Paramount.

Why did you produce it for theaters first instead of for television?

Because creatively I was ready. Ready to make a long film, with no commercials, a film that could go deep. It was our first feature-length documentary, released through MTV Films. It was released to 800 screens. It was a really big release for a documentary feature. It was interesting, because at the first marketing meetings with Paramount they made the decision, let's never talk about it as a documentary. You don't use that word, *documentary*.

Why was that?

Because at the test screenings, it was testing off the roof, and none of these people had ever gone to a theater to see a documentary. This is pre-*Fahrenheit 9/11*. But to these kids, it wouldn't even occur to them to go see a documentary, they just saw a good movie. So part of me was really torn. Part of me was saying, "I've been this advocate for documentary all these years. How could you not call it a

Shooting *Tupac: Resurrection*. Lazin worked with Tupac's mother, Executive Producer Afeni Shakur, to produce the film. "His mom had his photos and his poetry and his albums. I got access to the vault, stacks of phone numbers from girls, all kinds of great things. Then, I had to shape it so it had a dramatic flow, an arc, so that it felt like a movie. But certainly the story was there, and he really held it, he held the story."

Photo courtesy of Katy Garfield.

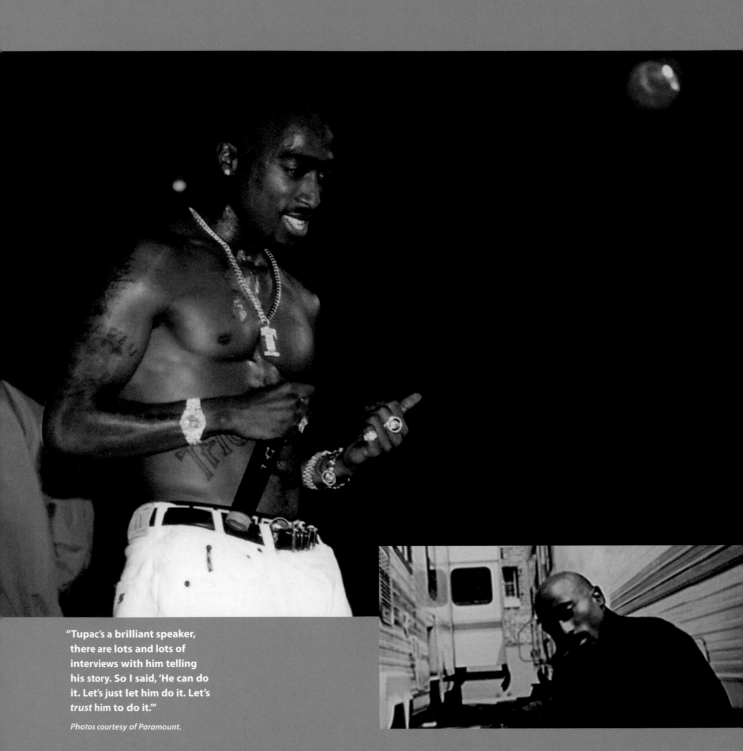

"Tupac's a brilliant speaker, there are lots and lots of interviews with him telling his story. So I said, 'He can do it. Let's just let him do it. Let's *trust* him to do it.'"

Photos courtesy of Paramount.

documentary?" But then part of me said, "You know what? It's going to reach a wider audience. It's still the film it is. Obviously, it's a documentary."

Why were you interested in making this film?

I had a concept to tell Tupac's story in his own words. And his mother, Afeni Shakur, had that same vision. A lot of people had wanted to make his life story.

How did you know that approach would work—an autobiography of a rap star, told in his own words, posthumously?

He's a brilliant speaker, there are lots and lots of interviews with him telling his story. So I said, "He can do it. Let's just let him do it. Let's *trust* him to do it." It took a lot of editing, a lot of shaping. There are a lot of interviews from a lot of different sources. So it was a year of doing that research, and gathering archival material. We had a lot of stuff in-house at MTV. His mom had his photos and his poetry and his albums. I got access to the vault, stacks of phone numbers from girls, all kinds of great things. Put together, it's a pretty traditional documentary film other than the whole concept of him telling his own story in his own words. Then, I had to shape it so it had a dramatic flow, an arc, so that it felt like a movie. But certainly the story was there, and he really held it, he held the story.

> *"Certainly the story was there, and he really held it, he held the story."*

How did it do?

It did well, seven-seven in box office [$7.7 million total domestic box office gross]. And it did extremely well on DVD. It's still selling very, very well. We had a big hit, platinum soundtrack, and a book. The book did really well. I'd like to do more films like that.

Avant-Garde Aesthetics

Music is obviously a big narrative component to the way you tell stories.

Fahrenheit 9/ll is a good example of a documentary that used music the way we've used music for a long time. It's just another tool at your disposal to tell stories. Sometimes we would use music that we would know our viewers would know the lyrics to, and know why we were using it, even though in the documentary we never came up on the lyrics. We work really hard to make the editing beautiful and precise. I'd see other documentaries on television, and I'd think, "It must be so easy to make that film and not have to kill yourself scoring it." Music is another reason why I think people watch MTV documentaries.

> *"I came to them saying, 'Let's do something that's about something.'"*

The PBS series *Alive From Off Center* was an incredibly innovative documentary series. You produced an episode for them, early on in your career. Can you tell me about it?

Oh, yes. That was a great documentary. It was a piece called *Seven Deadly Sins*. I actually hooked up with Neil Sealing, who was running it from a public television station in Minnesota. But I had wanted to do a piece with PBS. I was a big PBS fan.

Was that when you were at MTV?

Yes. I had wanted to do "MTV Meets PBS." It was lowbrow meets highbrow.

A surprising combination.

It was great in terms of publicity and press. We got a tremendous amount of press on it because, at that time, people were shocked: MTV and PBS? How could that be? But the thing that was so great about it was, Neil was so open-minded.

What was the subject matter?

It was on how the seven deadly sins are expressed through popular culture today, and how young people relate to them. For example, gluttony was bulimia. I think PBS put up half the money and we put up half the money. And we broke it into two parts, because we had a lot of rights acquisitions. I think MTV ran it as an hour, and PBS ran it as two half hours.

Had PBS and MTV ever worked together before?

PBS had already done something with MTV with the promo department. We had a really avant-garde approach, especially in the early days. That's where [MTV president] Judy McGrath came from, she ran the promo department. That stuff was beautiful, it was art. And they worked with, you know, Andy Warhol and Jean-Michel Basquiat. They had done a piece for *Alive From Off Center*, a series of MTV promos. So that's how the connection was originally made. I came to them saying, "Let's do something with some content, let's do something that's *about* something."

Why was it a successful collaboration?

They weren't afraid to push buttons, they weren't afraid to talk about religion. I remember we had a lot of press, and the reviewers didn't know how to wrap their heads around the program. Is it MTV? Is it PBS? What is it? Once again, we got our biggest support from teachers and from theologians.

Theologians supported the *Seven Deadly Sins*?

Yes! All these religious people who worked with young people loved it. Because they thought, "Oh my God, you're talking to young people about moral and ethical issues, and about *how to live your life.*" They watched the shows. That's always the biggest stumbling block, getting them to watch the shows. I know it was a great collaboration, because we both aired it at exactly the same time, and both our ratings were great. We both hit our audience with equal strength. And then we got a Cable Ace Award for it. That's one of the highlights for me, those kinds of collaborations with different partners.

maintain that with a series. I mean, people do it. *Frontline* is a really good example, I think, and *P.O.V.*

When you're producing an episode for a specific series, how do you foster the individuality of each episode? Is that something you get very involved with in each show?

Yes, we're pretty hands-on. Some shows require more input than others. A show for a series like *Cribs* or *Diary* doesn't need as much hand-holding as something like a *True Life* show does. I'm pretty hands-on when it comes to looking at the scripts—and they do have scripts; every single thing we do has a script.

When you are trying to get a project off the ground, what is your relationship to MTV?

My college professor Ron Alexander used to say you have to be a force of nature. It sounds so obvious! But, you know what? That's really what you have to be. It ended up being a gem of wisdom; I tell filmmakers that all the time. If you have a vision, or an idea, you have to use *all* your resources to make it happen. You have to bring it to the people that you think are going to be sympathetic to it, or who are going to be interested in it economically, or creatively, or people who just care about the subject matter.

Can you give me an example where you rallied champions to get a project you cared about financed?

A good example was a piece that I'm directing right now called, *I'm Still Here: Diaries of Young People Who Lived During the Holocaust*. A couple years ago—it was before I directed *Tupac: Resurrection*—I brought this to the heads of MTV and said, "I found this book written by Alexandra Zapruder called *Salvaged Pages: Young Writers' Diaries of the Holocaust*. She collected diaries written by young people; she found over 50 diaries written by young people during the Holocaust—peers of Anne Frank!" I asked the MTV heads, "Don't you think that would make a great documentary for MTV, the voices of young people telling about the Holocaust from

I'M STILL HERE

REAL DIARIES OF YOUNG PEOPLE WHO LIVED DURING THE HOLOCAUST

Kirsten Johnson

Cinematographer

Searching the Frame, Exposing a Vision

SINCE 1990, KIRSTEN JOHNSON HAS TRAVELED THE WORLD, SHOOTING and directing independent documentaries. She began her artistic career as an undergraduate at Brown University, where she studied painting, political science, and comparative literature. Johnson recalls "trying to put visual things together with political things … by making these terrible paintings with words in them. It wasn't quite *working*!" After graduating, she traveled to Africa to meet two Senegalese filmmakers, Ousmane Sembene and Djibril Diop Mambetty, whose work she was interested in. While in Africa, she worked on her first films. Soon after, Johnson became the first American to attend the French national film school—École Nationale Supérieure des Métiers de L'image et du Son—known as La Femis. There she studied cinematography and gained a deep appreciation for high aesthetic standards. Respected and beloved within the filmmaking community, Johnson now works throughout

Kirsten Johnson filmography

Cinematography

Election Day (TBD) (Quincy, Florida)
Bela Fleck: The Africa Project (TBD)
Slacker Uprising Tour (2005)
Fahrenheit 9/11 (2004)
Ladies First (2004)

Festival of the Unconquered
Hecate and Trinlay
A Charter School in the Bronx (2004)
Building to Extremes (2003)
Osama Bin Laden: The Opera (2003)
Deadline (2004)

Learing Outloud (2003)
Coming by Boat: Haitian Immigration
Teach the Children Well: Children and
   Terrorism (2002)
Life 360—"Secrets" (2002)

Men's Depression (2001)
Asylum (2004)
A Decade Under the Influence—
   Filmmaking in the 1970s (2003)
The Hamptons (2001)

Kirsten Johnson began her cinematography career in Paris, at La Femis, the French national film school. "'You'll never get in if you apply as a director,' I was told. 'You should figure out which other department you're interested in.' I was really interested in camerawork so I said, 'I'll try cinematography.'"

Photo courtesy of Big Mouth Productions.

the world as a director and a cinematographer, and she has often teamed up with leading political filmmakers such as Barbara Kopple, Raoul Peck, Kirby Dick, and Michael Moore.

For the directors and others she works with, she offers a combination of three traits that make her a rare find.

First, her international schooling brings her an appreciation of the fine arts that translates to an instinctive obsession for quality lighting and framing—an obsession more common among painters than journalistically trained cinematographers. As she describes it, "Often, the topics that people want to make documentaries about are questions of social difficulty, and I feel that giving audiences visual interest and pleasure allows them to stay connected and feel like they can cope with often very difficult, painful material. If everything is ugly and brutal, it's hard to take."

Second, she combines an artistic sensibility with an innate passion for the story, and a deep commitment to creating images that fully communicate themes and substance. The opening of the film *Deadline*, which Johnson shot and codirected with Katy Chevigny, feels as dramatic and striking as any feature film. "I wanted to film the image of the man's hands folded in his lap, or the way his foot was tapping on the floor, or the tension in his hands, and I wanted to make that separate from the specific prisoner, to indicate this sense of scale. By isolating the hands against the uniform that they're wearing, indicates that we're talking about prisoners, not just this one prisoner."

Third, Johnson's collaborative style—her humility, focus, generosity, and careful consideration of the subject—helps her to realize the directors' vision. "I like to connect *how* I'm shooting to *what* I'm shooting."

The success of this style is reflected in how she selects new projects: Johnson's filmography demonstrates her devotion to provocative documentary filmmaking. Furthermore, she's traveled to the ends of the earth to pursue this dedication: Her work has taken her to Senegal, France, China, Thailand, Malaysia, India, Brazil, Nicaragua, Morocco, Western Africa, and throughout Europe. At every location,

Johnson's cinematography captures a visual freshness. She also brings sensitivity to how audiences will view the people and the locations she represents. When she shot *Journey to the West,* also directed by Chevigny, a film about Chinese medicine and the relationship between China and the United States, the two developed a concept of creating "confusion" to upset viewers' expectations, and "break the clichés and exoticization that happen in our imagination of a place that we've never been to." Johnson explains, "I looked at a lot of Chinese painting before shooting, and I would frame the landscape in Monterey, California, to look like a Chinese painting. And then in China, I would look for a composition that was different from my idea of what China would be, but something that was much more familiar to me on a certain level."

Johnson has made many films that deal with difficult subject matter, from large-scale human tragedies to personal stories of endurance and suffering. "I worked with the Shoah Foundation and filmed over 200 interviews of Holocaust survivors. I've worked on a lot of criminal justice stories. *Bintou in Paris* is a documentary about African immigrants in Paris who were facing the question of female genital mutilation. I worked in Rwanda on a film about post-genocide issues. I always say, 'I'm going to do a comedy next!'"

While many of these harrowing stories have been told by other journalists, Johnson's approach to each is distinct. By offering a multifaceted character-driven story, her films describe the plight in the context of individual lives. "I think that there is a way in which, when you're actually with the people who have experienced incredibly difficult things, you go into a place of empathy and curiosity that allows you to cope to a certain extent." In the same way she bonds with directors, Johnson develops a personal connection with the subjects of her films. "It's often incredibly painful for people to talk about some of what they've experienced, and yet they have made some kind of choice to let themselves be filmed. In that arrangement of trust, I think there's a space for human attention."

Johnson describes a man who was giving an interview for the Shoah Foundation. "He clearly had a very uncomfortable relationship to talking about his experiences. He spoke in this completely monotone, flat voice, and initially, I thought, 'He isn't

Images from the film *Derrida*, about French literary critic and philosopher Jacques Derrida, which played at the 2001 Sundance Film Festival. "He had a very complex relationship to his image," Johnson explains. **"For years and years he didn't let himself be photographed. He wanted it to be about the ideas, and not about him as a person. We had all kinds of discussions over how it would be set up, so that we would rarely have filmed him directly."**

Courtesy of Jane Doe Films.

Can you give an example from the film?

I remember one of the first times we filmed an interview with him he said, "I'm just going to ask you one thing. I only want to be filmed in profile." So I said, "OK." Not exactly the way I like to set up an interview, but why not? When I set everything up, he came downstairs and he said, "You've done exactly what I told you not to do." And I said, "But I set it up to shoot in profile." And he said, "I meant the *left* profile!"

That sounds challenging. How did you work within such rigid constraints?

He was actually very generous and allowed us to spend time with him in his home, filming while he was writing, and talking on the phone, and organizing his work. He was an incredibly powerful presence, and someone who had such rigor in his daily life that it made you stand up even straighter in the way you held the camera. There was this incredible seriousness to his way of operating, and it was really nice, because it made me search for things with the camera in a different way than I ever had before.

There was a lot of experimentation in that project, and it gave me a lot of confidence in the different ways in which you can film what is real. It is just Jacques Derrida in his office, but where are you with the camera? Are you in his garden, filming him through the trees, through the window, into his office? Are you getting the detail of the way he puts the caps back on all his pens while he's talking on the phone? That experience of having the time—where no one was saying a thing and I was to be this unobtrusive presence—allowed me to be there for hours while he was in that space. It allowed for all kinds of searching. It was the beginning of me being comfortable with the silence of being a cameraperson, which is not my natural way of being in the world.

Cinematography and Directing:
Informing Filmmaking

When you join a new project, how do you begin?

I often ask directors to help me with this, to think about what the themes are that we're paying attention to. If we're talking about interactions between people across some kind of divide, then I start asking questions like: When do people touch each other? What are people's physical relationships to each other? Or it might be that the director is interested in portraying questions of trust. So, I'll pay particular attention to people's eyes and what they're watching and when.

You work as both a cinematographer and a director. Why?

Pretty early on, I decided I wanted to do both. After film school, I worked as a cinematographer for different people I'd gone to school with, and I also initiated my own projects that I directed. What I discovered in film school was that I loved working with other people, and I liked the difference of being a cinematographer and then being a director. They're distinctly different positions, and I think until you've done both of them you don't quite realize what the other person is up to. For me, it became very clear that the back and forth was really informing my film-making, and broadening me.

Tell me about your collaboration with Julia Pimsleur, Katy Chevigny, and the others at Big Mouth Productions.

I work independently, freelance, but they are my home base. I've shot several Big Mouth films, and Katy Chevigny, Julia Pimsleur, and Dallas Brennan have been incredible producers on my documentary work as director, *Innocent Until Proven*

Guilty and *Deadline*. The first project I did out of film school, I worked with Julia Pimsleur, who Katy Chevigny cofounded Big Mouth, and we got a commission to make a documentary about African immigrants in Paris who were facing the question of female genital mutilation. It's called *Bintou in Paris*. It was a short, 17-minute film.

Why was that concept of interest to you?

Female genital mutilation is illegal in France. At the time we made the film, some people had done the procedure to their girls while they were babies instead of waiting until they were pre-teens to avoid trouble with the law, but then a baby died, and there was a big hullabaloo.

From the experience I'd had in Senegal, I thought that making a documentary wasn't the solution in this case. I felt like making a melodrama, a film where there was a clear story, and a conflict with someone who was recognizable to people who was torn between all these different positions, would speak to people.

How did you approach that film cinematically?

I wanted to make everyone look really beautiful, because it's one of those topics where everyone says, "Oh, I don't want to see it." I worked with this wonderful cinematographer who was at La Femis with me named Nasr Djepa, and we shot the whole thing trying to make it as beautiful as possible.

I know it was a film festival hit. Did you secure distribution beyond that?

That film ended up being shown on television throughout Africa and in France. It was shown in health centers. It was an interesting hybrid. I wrote the screenplay based on interviews I had done with people about their experiences, and then, when we shot it with the actors, it turned out that many of the actors had actually experienced it firsthand, so there a nice back and forth to it, between what was documentary and what was fiction. The collaboration between Julia and I felt great, and it seemed like we could come to the United States and make more films together.

Why did you believe that melodrama was the right genre for *Bintou in Paris*?

Well, I think simply because it's a dramatic situation, and yet there has to be some-place where there's a little seduction in it. It needs something that gets people in and allows people to identify and, also, I think the melodrama creates a tiny bit of distance, so it's not too raw. The young mother is just gorgeous, and you wanted to watch it in this sensual way, but then there was this other dilemma going on underneath it.

It's important to you to create compelling visual images for the documentaries you work on, so that people are interested in watching them?

That's something I think about a lot. Often, the topics that people want to make documentaries about are questions of social difficulty, and I feel that giving audiences the visual interest and the visual pleasure allows them to stay connected and feel like they can cope with often very difficult, painful material. If everything is ugly and brutal, it's hard to take.

Of course, sometimes that *is* appropriate. Sometimes it's not about glamour, or creating a false relationship between things. But I think, to a great extent, people have been filmed in a way that makes them look more helpless or more ugly or more disenfranchised than they actually are. So I feel that searching for the humanity is also searching for the beauty, and that's part of what I try to do.

Profit and Nothing But!

***Profit and Nothing But!* is an examination of the profit motive and its impact on people's daily lives, on history, and on the future.**

Tell me about working with Raoul Peck.

Raoul Peck's a director that I loved working with! I worked with him on a documentary that he shot in Paris, New York, and Port-au-Prince, and I shot the New York part. It was called *Profit and Nothing But!* I had enormous respect for him as a filmmaker, and I was very excited to do a couple of days shooting with him in New York. It was one of those experiences that was almost revolutionary for me in the way I saw what one could do with a camera. We had this very complicated day organized, where we were going to shoot all over New York City. We started out on the day, and we got to the first location, and he says, "Oh, there's nothing happening with the light here. Let's go." And I said, "*What?!*"

Do you mean he would determine when to shoot at a specific location based on how striking the natural light was?

Yes. Usually in a documentary situation you only have so much money, and you only have so much time, and you shoot whatever is there when you get there. But, in fact, he had this incredible commitment to the light. It always had to be interesting, and if it wasn't, it wasn't worth shooting—even if the content was there, even if the people were there.

How did you accomplish that?

We ended up just crisscrossing Manhattan. When he first came to New York he worked as a taxi driver, so he had this incredible sense of how to get around Manhattan. We went up and down, back and forth, over and over. Every place we went, when there was something incredibly interesting happening with the light, that's when we could start to shoot.

Peck's aesthetic commitment superseded everything else. How did that affect your collaboration process?

It was an exhilarating feeling. For example, we would be shooting something like an outdoor market, or people running in the park, where the action was continuously happening. We were doing it all on tripod, and he would tell me what he was looking for, and I'd set up the frame. And then—and this is very different from most documentary directors—he would look at the frame and he'd say, "Hmmm," and he would move it slightly. And *every* time it was absolutely better than what

I had framed. And every time it would be this revelation for me. I would realize, "Oh my goodness. It's so much more interesting, what he set up."

Did you eventually get into sync with what he was looking for?

It became this challenge for me: I'm going to set up a shot that Raoul doesn't need to move. I'd think, "Here's what I *think* is a good frame, but let me move around a little bit and find what might make Raoul a little happier."

I think, out of the several days we worked together, maybe three or four times I pulled off a shot that he didn't want to move. I was so proud! It was really thrilling. That level of aesthetic standards was really quite wonderful for me.

Can you describe the subject of the film, and how it was possible for him to be so deliberate with his shot setups?

Like most of his documentaries, it was an essay kind of film. It wasn't a verité situation, in that we were not there following predetermined characters, and there was action happening that we couldn't stop. We were filming life going on, and he was looking to have ideas expressed through a specific vision of what society is. And he was contrasting three very different societies. But to a great extent, it was his point of view on those places. The film is narrated by him, but there's also this very strong, specific visual sense that is Raoul's that comes through. It's like one of those things where you *know* you're contributing to it, but you're basically trying to express this point of view.

That sounds like a challenging collaboration. Why is that appealing to you?

As you work with a person like that, you learn more aesthetically, and you start to realize they like having somebody in the foreground, they like having something dissonant happening in the frame. Little by little, you start to get their aesthetic. But certainly, with someone who has such a strong and clear sense, as Raoul does, it takes some time.

Asylum

Asylum **is a short documentary about a Ghanian woman named Baba who searches for her father. The sequence of events after she finds him is intense, dramatic, and horrifying to American audiences, as he insists that she follow his wishes, that include arranged marriage and female genital mutilation. Baba's attempt to find refuge in the United States demonstrates the need for reform of the immigration system.**

You collaborated with Sandy McLeod and Gini Reticker on *Asylum*.

We were very happy that *Asylum* was nominated for an Academy Award!

Yes, congratulations.

Thanks. It was my first time working with Sandy, and both she and Gini had never been to Ghana before. They had this idea that the film they were going to make was going to be made up of many fictional set ups. We were going to cast little girls and film them at home and at school in set scenes. And I said to them, "I think we have to save a lot of time for just shooting in a documentary kind of way. For example, we can go to a school, but then let's film what's actually happening there." They were open to that idea. So we had this schedule that was supposed to be half and half—created dramatic moments and observational documentary work.

How did that plan work out?

It was fantastic, because the first day, and the first 20 feet that we drove in the car, I thought, "Oh, I wish we could stop the car, because I really want to shoot that." And, at exactly that moment, Sandy said, "Stop the car!" And she and I had this spot-on aesthetic, where we knew what kinds of things we were looking for, but it would be very spontaneous. So we'd recognize that the woman walking by with the sewing machine on her head in front of the red wall would be the shot that would express our idea. Sandy would get it, and I would get it, and we'd say, "Stop

Over the past two decades, Johnson has shot films on three continents. This image is from *Asylum*, one of many collaborations between Johnson and producer/director Gini Reticker.

Photo courtesy of Gini Reticker.

the car." She wouldn't even tell me what I was supposed to shoot. We'd both seen it, and we'd know. So, that was really fun, because we developed a language of filming that incorporated these painted signs that exist all over Ghana. They have all these painted signs, and they're really evocative. Many of them are images of women, like a woman going "*Shhh*!" with her finger to her lips—things that could relate to the story. You'd see that sign and say, "Okay, get that." So that was a real pleasure, to find someone's whose aesthetic exactly matched mine.

It sounds like a very successful collaboration.

We almost didn't need to communicate. Gini, Sandy and I knew what we were looking for. There were some hysterical moments. I remember, we were at the restaurant at the airport, and I went to the bathroom, and I came out of the bathroom and I said, "Umm … I need the camera." In the bathroom, I noticed there was a window with a screen on it, and there was bougainvillea brushing up against the screen of the window, and it was beautiful. So I said, "Give me the camera," went back to the bathroom, got the shot, came back out, and that shot's in the film. It's one of those things: You're in the zone of knowing what the material is that works for the film and it may come at any moment.

Was your creative input carried out in the final film, beyond the shooting?

That's one of the films where it's clear from the way it was edited that the editor really understood the way I was shooting, which is rare. It was cut by Kate Taverna.

With the Ghana case, with *Asylum*, we became very interested in tying in the theme in a visually graphic way, so we were looking for the signs. It might be a sign for a manicure shop, but the hands are being gently held by another hand, so that speaks to our theme.

A lot of times I'll be filming with a set of about six different themes that I'm paying attention to in the actual interactions. For example, if there's an argument between two people, but in the background there's a young child watching, I'll frame it with the body language of the arguing people in the foreground and the child watching it, so that the scene clearly relates to one of our themes.

Where does the editor come in? Do you meet with her or him?

The editor, when they're fantastic—like Kate Taverna or Carol Dysinger—will see that and know that's what I was doing in that moment. Hopefully, the directors have that same conversation with the editor about themes and what's going on in the footage, but sometimes an editor may intuitively understand what the film's about and they're looking for something to speak to that theme and, *boom*, there it is.

Tell me about working with Michael Moore.

I love working with Michael. I actually came into *Fahrenheit 9/11* very close to the end.

Republican Governor Ryan surprised the country when he suspended enforcement of the death penalty in the state of Illinois. "I now favor a moratorium, because I have grave concerns about our state's shameful record of convicting innocent people and putting them on death row," Ryan said. "I cannot support a system which, in its administration, has proven to be so fraught with error and has come so close to the ultimate nightmare, the state's taking of innocent life. Thirteen people have been found to have been wrongfully convicted."

Photo courtesy of Big Mouth Productions.

Jones is one inmate in this situation, but we have 2,000,000 people in prison, and they are all human beings. By isolating the hands against the uniforms that they're wearing, that says we're talking about all prisoners, not just this one prisoner.

Editors Carol Dysinger and Kate Hirson were fantastic in the way they understood those kinds of details. There's a sequence later in the film that is just about the prosecutor's position, and the litany of pain that people are experiencing. One thing that we picked out were all these hand gestures, so it was the prosecutor gesturing with his hand, and the person sitting there. There are all these very specific gestures that indicated people's pain, expressed through the hands.

How did that concept develop?

It's a combination of me shooting it with the knowledge that I'm shooting this closeup of a hand now because this is the place where I see the most pain expressed, and then having these wonderful editors who say, "OK, we've actually got 16 shots of hands that will tell more about the level of pain people experience than having someone cry over and over." So there's a very formal intention. We were able to go back and forth between the sequences that involved that formal imagery and the more verité courtroom scene, where you're filming what's *happening* in a narrative film style.

When did that concept come to you?

I'm very influenced by Patricio Guzman's film, *The Battle of Chile*. There was an extraordinary cameraperson, Jorge Müller Silva, who shot an amazing scene where, basically, there's an important officer in the navy who is loyal to Allende, who gets assassinated. They're on the cusp of the coup, and all these military officers are gathered for this funeral, but everybody's on one side or another. The cameraman very slowly moves through the crowd and finds the telling detail on each person that indicates which side they're on. It's so gorgeous. It's all 16 millimeter black and white. Silva slowly searches up and down, and once he's found it on the person—for example, someone's knotting his tie really tight—he'll pan out until he

Buddy Squires

Cinematographer

Seeing Intelligently

BUDDY SQUIRES EASILY MAKES THE SHORT LIST OF LEADING DIRECTORS of photography in documentary production. His exceptionally beautiful cinematography is often lit as formally and meticulously as a fine painting. He is perhaps best known for the work he's done with director Ken Burns for PBS, on public television programs such as *Brooklyn Bridge, The Civil War, Mark Twain, Jazz, Unforgivable Blackness: The Rise and Fall of Jack Johnson,* and numerous others. He is also well respected, however, for his contributions to cinema verité feature-length documentaries that are often seen at the Sundance Film Festival or on HBO's *America Undercover*. He takes a different approach to every project, from carefully set-up studio shoots, and his inventive filming of historical still photographs, to time-lapse shots and event-based verité work.

Squires shoots to serve the story, to build the film concept visually in a manner that the *Hollywood Reporter* described as an "exquisitely understated style." Many film editors have remarked how Squires's innovative approach to shooting is invaluable in providing them with ways of pulling the story

Buddy Squires filmography

Cinematographer

After Innocence (2005)

Ring of Fire: The Emile Griffith Story (2005)

People's Poetry: A Populist Bacchanal (2004)

Broadway: The American Musical (2004)

Unforgivable Blackness: The Rise and Fall of Jack Johnson (2004)

Happy to Be Nappy and Other Stories of Me (2004)

Reporting America at War: Episode Two, Which Side Are You On? (2003)

Columbia: A Celebration (2003)

Beauty in a Jar (2003)

The Boys of 2nd Street Park (2003)

Crime & Punishment (2002)

Miss America (2002)

Indie Sex: Taboos (2001)

The Merchants of Cool (2001)

Mark Twain (2001)

Richard Rodgers: The Sweetest Sounds (2001) (director of photography)

▶ **Cinematographer Buddy Squires, followed by opium workers, climbs a hill in the Golden Triangle in Burma with full camera gear and tripod. "Cameras are big and bulky, people are big and bulky. A film crew is a little bit of an army when it moves in. But at the same time, one has to try to disappear as much as possible, and be as unobtrusive as possible. When one is allowed into the important, intimate, moving moments of other people's lives, it's a very privileged place to be."**

Photo courtesy of Buddy Squires.

together in the cutting room. Academy Award-nominated director Edet Belzberg calls him, "Simply, the best."

Squires believes that a cinematographer's mission is to deliver images that add meaning and depth to the narrative, furthering the story line. His commitment is to realize and translate the director's vision, and fulfill the film's narrative intention. What separates passable camera work from Squires's artful cinematography is the careful observation and understanding he uses when approaching the search for a "telling image." Before shooting commences, Squires consults with the director to problem solve and determine the best way to create dramatic moments in the film, not merely capture the action. Squires conceived of this way of working to insure that the larger themes of the story will be incorporated into his filmmaking. Later, at the shoot, he identifies what's interesting based on this pretuned filter, determining how what he sees contributes to the character development or narrative story arc as envisioned by the director. "Sometimes I will scan the whole frame and ask, 'What is it that you're *seeing*?' One has to be responsible for every choice, and every frame is a choice."

With Ken Burns, Squires originated an approach to shooting historical documentaries that has often been imitated, he says. It's a slow-paced style designed to convey history through the use of photos, paintings, rare archival drawings and documents, interviews, and the use of famous voiceover talent. Of his work with Burns, Squires says, "I have never totaled it up, but many hours of public television time and DVD shelves have been filled with it." As an early collaborator and cofounder of Burns's documentary production company, Florentine Films, Squires helped respond to the unusual question, "How do you rephotograph a photograph to tell a story?"

Over the years, Squires's stylish answer has transcended the limitations of working with antique photos, and inanimate objects like the Statue of Liberty and the Brooklyn Bridge, to speak to viewers in the most dramatic terms. His revealing style transports audiences into nonfiction stories with extraordinary verisimilitude,

Style that Tells the Story

Over the years, Squires has employed many novel approaches to cinematography by experimenting with camera technology and taking calculated creative risks to inform the story through style.

On *The Donner Party*, he filmed a turning wagon wheel in slow-motion and it became a visual metaphor for the exertion and struggle of immigration. On *Brooklyn Bridge*, Squires took still pictures of the bridge throughout the day, then Ken Burns and editor Amy Stechler used his photographic images as well as a time-lapse film sequence over Frank Sinatra's vocals as an eloquent transition between the two sections of the film—history and symbolism. Here, Squires shares two techniques he's used on different projects to facilitate visual storytelling.

Using a Moving Extended Exposure

On *Las Vegas*, a film for the PBS series *American Experience*, Squires was tasked with creating an imaginative way to communicate the mood of the familiar desert city.

"Recently I've been working with Stephen Ives of Insignia Films on a project he's doing on the history of Las Vegas," Squires explains. "We were in Las Vegas and Ives was trying to get a sense of the energy of the place and the lights, and how that all played into the glitz. Of course we've all seen a million images of Las Vegas."

In trying to come up with a novel way to capture the city and its aura, Squires thought of the unique experience of time in Vegas—with clockless casinos and restaurants open all day and all night.

"It interests me to use tools that weren't necessarily available ten years ago, so I said, 'Maybe we should try doing a *moving* time-lapse.' I was working with the field producer at the time, and I just grabbed my film camera, and held it in the front windshield of a van as a test. We did a drive down the Las Vegas Strip rolling at one-second exposure, meaning one second per frame—so it's a full second of exposure [instead of 24 frames per second]—for an entire trip up and back the Strip, having that shutter open the entire time.

By photographing the famed Vegas Strip in this way, Squires delivered unusual semi-abstract imagery that appears smudged, colorful, and almost ghost-like. "I was using what's really a still photographing tool, which is the long exposure, and then applying that to the motion picture realm. The result was this wonderful, streaky, impressionistic view of Las Vegas—an extended exposure time-lapse. This shot couldn't possibly have been captured in real time, because it was a nonliteral sense of the place, its energy, motion, glitz, and lights."

Using Pixelation

On Ken Burns's *The Statue of Liberty*, Squires served as coproducer and cinematographer. In one memorable sequence, he collaborated with filmmaker Peter Hutton to employ pixelation, which he'd seen Hutton use very effectively on a film he'd made about artist Red Grooms.

Pixelation, or stop-frame animation, is a technique in which people, objects, or both are filmed one, two, or several frames at a time, moved incrementally, then filmed again, moved again, and so on. In the pixelation sequence Squires describes here, he had Hutton move the camera from place to place, shooting a few frames whenever he changed his location. The result was a hyperspeed tour of the Statue of Liberty.

"Peter did this wonderful sequence using an old Bolex and a little hand trigger. With this technique, you're allowing motion to happen within the frame. So if I did a pixelation of this room, I could set up a camera right here and you'd see all the motion in this room scurry about. Depending upon the shutter speed that you used, it would be a different look. So if you used a 1/16th of a second exposure, each motion of each person would be very crisp, Keystone Kop-like. If you did a two-second exposure per frame, everything that moved would be a blur moving through the frame.

"In this particular case the camera was on a tripod. The way Peter was using it was really more like taking the action apart and storyboarding it: You buy your ticket. You get on the boat. You take the boat over to the Statue. You get off the boat. You stand in line to get to the stairs. You go up the stairs. You get to the top. You look out the window. You come back down. You buy a hot dog. We shot a couple seconds of each activity."

Here again, as in the case of Las Vegas, the problem was shooting a location very familiar to tourists, and doing so in a way that made it seem fresh and new. The use of pixelation makes the film tour of the statue both foreign and familiar, much like one might experience it on a first visit after seeing it for decades in pictures.

"I've stolen the technique many times since," Squires says, "but I don't think it's ever had that same excitement. It's something Peter did really well."

It's the same thing when you use a tripod and when you don't use a tripod. What is being *communicated*? Al Maysles would say, never use a tripod. Al would say, never put up a light. I totally respect him for that; for his style of filmmaking, that's absolutely true. Al and I have had public panel discussions about this and I said, well, it depends what you're doing. I have done many, many films, including two seasons on an NBC series, where we never set up a light and we never used a tripod, and it was a wonderful, wonderful experience.

You seem to love to shoot verité.

Yes, I do.

And yet you've had a long-term collaboration with Ken Burns, whose films are definitely not cinema verité.

"A film crew is a little bit of an army when it moves in."

Probably four years ago, the Academy of Motion Picture Arts and Sciences in L.A. put together a cinematographer's panel. It was Al Maysles, me, Ricky Leacock, and one or two other people. And all these things came up, including Al saying he never uses lights and you never should ask a question. People in the audience were berating me, saying, "I'm so sick of your beautiful images." But, as I said then and I would say again, if one's wish is to tell the story of the Civil War, I can't tell that with a cinema verité film, hanging out watching people today. If the Civil War is the story you want to tell, then you have to figure out, how am I going to serve that story? And if that means putting people in front of a camera in a quiet room with some lights and all the apparatus around them, then that's what it is.

Ken's primarily making history films, and the heart of those films is somebody saying, let me tell you a story about a long time ago in a galaxy far, far away.... How do you let that story emerge, with little else getting in the way? One wants to create a situation where you can almost get into the imagination of the person telling the story, and eliminate distractions. For the most part, unlike a verité film, you're not interested where they live, or in knowing what their kitchen looks like, because it's not about that. It's about the story they have to tell you about something that happened in some other time and place. But don't say that they're not visual, because they're entirely visual. Otherwise, you're doing a radio show.

Becoming Invisible

Documentary producers often refer to the "fly-on-the-wall" shooting technique. How do you do your job as a cameraman while allowing reality to unfold before you, unaffected by your presence?

When one is allowed into the important, intimate, moving moments of other people's lives, it's a very privileged place to be. And one has to be incredibly careful not to trample on that and destroy their moment, whatever it happens to be. It can't be about you, it's got to be about them.

Cameras are big and bulky, people are big and bulky. A film crew is a little bit of an army when it moves in. But at the same time, one has to try to disappear as much as possible, and be as unobtrusive as possible. And that also comes from acting with confidence, moving with confidence, being respectful, but knowing where you can go and how you get there, when you can push and when you can't push, and whose turf you're on.

If you're doing neurosurgery, it's hard to get in there to see what you need to see, and you can't in any way violate what the chief surgeon dictates is the safety of the situation. But you still have to be able to get in. If little Amy is getting her new heart and is having her fourth birthday party, and you're there to shoot it, well, that's great that you're there to shoot it, but you'd better not get in the way of her birthday party. You don't want her party to not be a party all of a sudden, because you won't have anything to shoot. It's about being calm enough. But even if you're moving really fast, and running all over the place, somehow you're not calling too much attention to yourself. You're not making such a scene that you're a distraction. The minute you do that, the minute you take over, you've lost.

Squires shooting a scene with renowned primatologist Jane Goodall. "Years ago, I was doing a film in Africa that Karen Goodman and Kirk Simon were making," Squires says. "They were interested in the similarity between chimps and humans. One of the best pieces of advice Karen gave me was… 'You don't have to worry about covering each moment,' Because that wasn't the way that film was going to be edited. That was very liberating. Getting good direction is key."

Courtesy of Buddy Squires.

Handling Pressure, Taking Risks

In most verité shooting scenarios, there's a lot of spontaneous decision making. How do you determine what to respond to?

It is all problem solving. How do you find images that become the visual equivalent to the problem you're trying to solve?

Do you feel pressure?

Always, and never. Of course, there is good creative tension. Tension focuses one's energies. And yet, one also wants to be entirely calm. You don't want to be freaking out. If you're freaking out, you're not going to be focused, you're not going to be mentally focused, you're not going to be paying attention to where you are. That's very important, this word *attention*—you've got to pay attention to what it is you're *seeing*. It sounds so stupid, but that's all it is, it's about paying attention, looking, and seeing intelligently.

Particularly in verité work, you've got a huge amount of technical stuff which you have to be on top of: aperture and focus; do you have the right film stock? Is it the right exposure? Is it the right tape stock? Where am I in this roll of tape? What's my soundperson doing? You know, all those little details. At the same time you cannot let that interfere with your ability to see and perceive what you're doing. One of the great fears is, "That was a great scene—oh, hell, I wasn't rolling because something happened."

It is the verité work that is in some ways the most challenging. When it is an event that's happening in that moment, and that moment is here and it's gone, the interpretation you give to it absolutely determines what that scene is, what that sequence is, and how it works or doesn't work. You don't want to blow it. You don't want to miss it, but the only way you're not going to blow it is by having confidence that you've got it. It's a little bit like being an athlete. You train and train and train so that when the time comes, and you have to stand in the batter's box in the World Series, you know you're going to do your best and swing or not swing at the pitch; you have to know your stuff.

There's a ton of pressure, but you can't do good work if you pay too much attention to the pressure. But you might not do very good work if you don't pay any attention to it, if you're too lax and too unfocused.

How do you prepare for a verité shoot?

Preparing is just about working. It's about being in practice and knowing your tools. You don't show up to a scene with a new camera you've never used before, or a new technology, and say, "Well, I'll figure it out." I've actually done that a few times, but you try not to. You try to know your tools. You try to have done your homework, and then it's the same thing as taking a big exam. You try to know the technology you're working with, know the territory you're working with, have some understanding of why you're there.

What advice do you have for shooting a long-term project?

It's important to look at dailies, when possible. To watch the films, and to know that it's all a little mysterious. It's all a little supernatural.

You told me earlier that part of your process involves taking creative risks. Why is it important to take risks?

If one pays attention to the great documentary films, they're filled with those moments. In *Gimme Shelter* there is that famous sequence shot onstage where Jagger is seen in the foreground, and a man is getting more and more wasted on the opposite side of the stage. [The camera person] had the presence of mind to put Mick Jagger out of focus, and to focus on this fellow on the opposite side of the stage. And it's a wonderful thing to be so present in a moment that you can ignore the great superstar because what's happening is happening right here, in front of you.

Certainly, one of the best examples of that is in *Dont Look Back*; that wonderful sequence where Dylan is at the typewriter writing and Joan Baez is off to the side strumming guitar. I think it was Penne [D A Pennebaker] shooting; it had to be Penne the way that he senses what's going on in that room. It's magical, somebody really present when something is going on: this guy writing a song sitting at the typewriter, and this woman sitting over there strumming the guitar, and some other people hanging around, what that tells you about their world and that moment in time. One always wants to be present enough to get to those places. And if Al Maysles says he never asks a question, he doesn't, because that's his process. That's what he does. The trick is to find that, to believe in it, to stick with it, not to get nervous and change gears.

Do you always follow your instincts?

Yes. I think that that's really important for anyone who is in some way involved with the world of art. And it would be very pretentious to call a lot of what we do "art." A lot of it is crap, but great art does come from following one's instincts. So you have to have faith in yourself—because if one doesn't have faith in oneself, one can't make a decision. And ultimately it is the decisiveness—right or wrong—such as choosing to focus on the wasted guy in the background and not on Mick Jagger.

"It's all a little mysterious. It's all a little supernatural."

Are there ever negative consequences in following that philosophy?

Now, that's a great thing about making films either for oneself or with a group of people one collaborates with—you don't have to worry about getting yelled at by some angry producer: "What the hell? What do you mean, you're not paying attention to Mick Jagger?" So that, too, becomes a question, whether one is serving one's own vision or serving what you think your producer or director wants.

It's a valid question. If you're working for people, they're hiring you, they're paying you money, you owe them the respect to at least try to do what they want to do. But you also owe yourself the respect to do what you feel is right. That's the tricky part. I've gotten most screwed up when I've done stuff that didn't quite feel right to me because I thought it was what somebody else wanted me to do. I almost have to go through it and say, "OK, I hear what they're saying." Then you can present it back to someone and say, "What you said is this, but what I really think you mean is this. How about if we do it this way?"

So there's an aspect of negotiation and collaboration. I spend a lot of my time interpreting what other people say, and it often isn't the letter of what they say that matters, it is the spirit of what they say. One can get trapped following the letter if it doesn't make sense, if it doesn't somehow fit one's own idea of how something should be done.

Collaboration and Communication

Can you tell me how you interpret what a director is looking for?

It happens every day, literally. It is a process of talking about their vision for the film, coming up with the wagon wheels, coming up with the driving time-lapse shots, or the handheld walking pixelation time-lapse shot. It's hearing someone's idea of what it is they're interested in having happen, and finding a way to make that work. People say, "Well, I want it to be like this." And it's really not quite what the director said that matters, but what they mean. So it is all interpretative, very interpretative.

When you are working on a shoot, how important is communication?

Communication is obviously crucial with the people that one is working with. It's different, depending on how long one has worked with somebody. One of the things that's often said by people that Ken and I work with is, "You guys don't say anything, but things seem to happen." It's all very quick. We don't talk, we don't need to—because there are too many decades of history. We *know*. It doesn't mean everything's perfect; it doesn't mean I won't get a phone call: "You know, I was looking at what we did here and I thought maybe…" But that's fine, that's absolutely part of it. You have to be willing to admit that you make mistakes.

So, even with Ken, sometimes you misread each other? And you ask for his feedback?

Absolutely. You have to go in and honestly ask people what they think. And if they say, "Well, I wasn't so happy with this," don't freak out and get defensive, say, "What is it?" and be open. Doesn't mean you have to agree. One has one's own point of view. But at least hear what the people you trust are saying.

So you make mistakes?

Of course not! *I* don't make mistakes.

Oh, they have run the gamut, from the deeply distressing, opening the wrong side of the magazine and burning a roll of film type mistakes, which I've suffered my share of. I won't go into too much detail about that. It's happened. One of the things I dislike about shooting video is that it's not all that difficult, working in a frenetic, frantic situation, to end up where one of the switches gets out of sequence or doesn't trigger, and all of a sudden you realize you haven't been rolling the couple of minutes you thought you were rolling—in that brain surgery that you're not getting. You can't say, "Would you mind opening that up again?" I make mistakes in lighting all the time. I should have backed that off a little more, I should have brought that in a little bit more. You have to be willing to take criticism, and to give it to oneself.

Buddy Squires and Ken Burns were college friends and long-time collaborators. "In the beginning I did everything," Burns says. "Pre-Internet, I went to every archive, I shot every shot. But I didn't always do the interviews; Buddy Squires did interviews, too."

Photo by Jerome Liebling, courtesy of Florentine Films.

Creative Choices

As a cinematographer, your technical choices in part guide the creative possibilities for the editor. How do you decide when to use a single camera instead of a two cameras?

I actually don't like shooting multiple-camera situations. I'd much prefer to be in a single-camera situation.

Why is that?

With a single camera, there is that sense of real time. There's something about the continuity, about continuous action, that's very different than cutting back and forth between two camera angles.

Give me an example of a scene you shot that was strengthened by using a single camera.

There's a film that I worked on, the title is *After Innocence*. It's Jessica Sanders's film about what happens to people who have been released on DNA evidence after they've spent ten or 15 years in prison, and what one's life is like afterward.

When we were shooting in Philadelphia, we spent a couple of days with one of the men who'd been exonerated. His sometimes-girlfriend—I was never quite sure of the relationship—invited us to come over and have some food and hang out. We were also shooting. All of a sudden, at the dinner table, the two of them got into this heavy duty discussion about what life was like for him now, and what had happened in prison. I plopped myself on the corner of the table—one of them was here [points to the left end of the table] and one here [points to the right end of the table]. It was all about trying to be present, so thankfully there was just one camera. But I had to divide my energies between the two of them.

I asked myself, "Am I interested in what's being said, in terms of seeing it?" Knowing full well that Mark, my great soundman, had all the sound of the room.

But am I interested in what's being *said*, or am I interested in how that's being *received*? Or am I interested in the energy and motion between the two? That's a lot of what guides me.

Because as much as I say it's about the image, it *is* about the image, but you have to know and sense which image is likely to be the most telling at any given moment. It may well not be the person speaking. It may have nothing to do with the person speaking. I think anybody who doesn't listen has no business working with live humans.

Can you tell me about a recent shoot when you had to use two cameras? I imagine sometimes it's necessary.

Yes. I haven't seen it because it's just been finished. It's called *Ring of Fire: The Emile Griffith Story*, and it's about the boxer Emile Griffith who became well known around 1962. He killed Benny "Kid" Paret in the ring on live national television. And he's got a dramatic story to his life. Griffith himself was severely mugged in the '70s and suffered some damage from that.

"It's about looking at the whole frame, about being attentive

Dan Klores, who's the director of that film, and his partner, Ron Berger, brought Emile together with the son of Paret, Benny Jr., who was three or two at the time his dad was killed. He lives in Miami, had never met Emile.

The last day of shooting, the plan was to bring Emile and Benny Jr. together. This occurred in Central Park. I have no idea how they cut it—they may have cut it as the continuous shot, but we indeed had two cameras there in order to cover everything. I just remember being there, and we had two different cameras walking in, one with each of the two people, backing up with each person. And then that sense of *meeting*. Just that feeling of the two of them meeting, and embracing, and crying. Here's the guy who killed your father, and what's he going to say? It's that sort of forgiveness that's flowing between the two of them; a very genuine thing. And just how you see that, and whose tears are you looking at? At every second you have to decide, I'm going to go *here*, I'm going to go *there*. We were completely still, trying to be Zen-like with the situation. I know I just need to see him, but I also need to know what's going on over here [gestures forward, in the periphery] and I have to know when I'm going to move between the two. You have to make a decision.

How do you decide how to frame a shot?

Within a frame, it's about looking at the whole frame, about being attentive to what's in that frame, and not assuming, because it's there, it's OK. Like, if that color doesn't fit in that part of the frame, well, get that color out of the frame. If this image doesn't feel right, well, do something about it. Sometimes I will just scan the whole frame—"Is that what I want?" One has to be responsible for every choice, and every frame is a choice. You are responsible, whether you happen to be or not, for what's within that frame. And also, ultimately, for what's not in the frame. If it's a mistake that it's not there, then *you've* left it out.

What about lockdown versus handheld shoots?

In a lot of the work that I do I never set up a tripod. It's all handheld. I was the lead DP on an NBC series which was a nonfiction version of *Law and Order* called

to what's in that frame."

Crime and Punishment that ran for two years, directed by Bill Guttentag. It focused on the lives of assistant district attorneys in San Diego, and we followed them all the way through a given case, from the preparation of going to trial, to the trial itself, to the verdict, and the aftermath. We never once used a tripod in any of the material when we were following the assistant DAs around. If we were in a courtroom shooting a courtroom scene, that was different. Many films that I do now, if they're verité films, we use no tripod, no lights. Well, not too many lights, anyway, depending on the situation. But it is what serves it.

Can you elaborate on how that decision was made, to shoot handheld? Was it your decision as the lead DP, or does the network director get involved?

It was Bill's idea. I can't vouch for it because I wasn't there, but I believe he took it to [*Law and Order* Executive Producer] Dick Wolf. And I think the idea was that the fictional show, *Law and Order*, very much tries to have that handheld you-were-just-there feel to it. *Crime and Punishment* was basically taking the "order" part of *Law and Order* and doing a verité series, but cutting it as if it were a *Law and Order* show. I don't think Wolf Films and NBC had any great interest in having a documentary on the air. I think they felt there was as much drama in the actual goings-on as there was in something they could write, and they were willing to take that risk.

It ran for two seasons, it did very well. I think the numbers were extremely good. It was not a reality show by any stretch of the imagination, although it was much more reality than any reality show. But there was nothing set up, there was nothing preplanned. You couldn't plan a verdict. You didn't plan how the evidence is going to come out. And our place was always secondary. We didn't ever ask anybody—I certainly never asked anyone, "Hold on, wait, can you ask that again? Can you do it over?" You don't do it, because they'd throw us out. They've got a job to do, and it's a really important job. You're dealing with these very powerful human dramas. It was a great thing to do. It was a great way to merge these worlds [of documentary and fictional television].

John Dowdell, colorist, working on a film at Technicolor
Labs. "John is god," Squires
says. "He has color-corrected
more than half of what I've
done in my life, and I love
John. He'll save my ass."

Photo courtesy of Magnet Media, Inc.
From **Zoom In.**

Lighting, Subtlety, and Storytelling

Tell me about your approach to lighting.

I try to bring that same attention to light, to situations where you have no light, where you can't control it but you can still control where you go and how you use whatever's available.

Can you contrast your approach to shooting film versus shooting video?

It's different to light video than film, but it's not more challenging. It's actually easier. What I mean by that is that you have the feedback of looking at a monitor. We know how it's going to respond. It's not really up to what happens in the lab. That said, I think film is a more forgiving, flexible medium. Film still has tremendous latitude and tremendous ability to handle a massively wide contrast range. What one can do with a good negative, with even a half decent negative these days, is astonishing.

Sometimes, contrary to popular belief, one needs more lights with video. I think there's a subtlety that exists within film—and you can see, a lot of the lighting I do for Ken is very subtle. I tend to use a little bit more edge light in video, a little more separation, because you don't really quite trust it to go in the same way. Certainly for pure, raw image quality nothing touches film. But it all depends on the situation. I love the image of film, and yet it's not always the right thing. You need to use the tool that's right for the medium that you're working with.

When you're on the shoot, how do you confirm with the director that you're making the right choices?

With Ken Burns, there's so much history to draw upon that it's all evolutionary. And it may be a little tighter, a little wider, a little something. Ken doesn't want a distinctly different style for the stories he's done, because even though his films are not all the same story, they're being told using some of the same tools. So there's a lot of re-creating that look.

Albert Maysles

Cinematographer

Being Present
and Experiencing

THE LIST OF EXTRAORDINARY PEOPLE TO WHOM CINEMATOGRAPHER/ director Albert Maysles has gained intimate access and captured on film at historic moments includes John F. Kennedy, Muhammed Ali, the Rolling Stones, artists Christo and Jeanne-Claude, Truman Capote, Sophia Loren, Fidel Castro, Warren Beatty, The Beatles, Marlon Brando, and too many others to list. "Making films has brought me in contact with big minds and small minds," he told me. "And the small minds are sometimes bigger than the big minds in many ways." The closeness Maysles feels to all his subjects is readily apparent, yet, this has not prevented him from exposing character flaws, something that critics comment on frequently. Two seemingly contradictory adjectives—*empathetic* and *unsparing*—are often used to describe Maysles's portrayal of real-life characters.

Maysles often uses film (and now video) along with his skills as a nonfiction storyteller to expose concealed meaning in what would otherwise be

with Russians, I went off with this wind-up 16 mm Keystone camera. CBS said, "Look, it's another week before you actually go to Russia. Here's a roll of film. Shoot it, and allow enough time when you come to New York so we can process it and give you a critique." That was my training. The deal was somewhat lopsided, but I had the camera, and they supplied me with the footage.

What was the deal you struck with CBS?

I would eventually own everything, but they would show whatever they thought they needed and pay me a dollar a foot. They used 14 feet. I got $14 for my effort. I owned the stuff. So I took it and went to WGBH in Boston, where I was living, and said, "Look, I've got this interesting material of mental hospitals in Russia, and if you allow me to use some of your equipment to put it together, I'd like you to show it." That would be the deal. They agreed, and they showed the film. As I was editing the film, they had a visitor from a pharmaceutical company interested in appealing to psychiatrists, and they said, "We know you're making this film, and we'd like to make 50 prints of it when you're finished. We'll pay you $2000." So already I made a deal. The trip itself cost me $1700, a thousand of which was for the air ticket. The rest, the $700, was for a hotel room. In those days travel was so terribly restricted, and you had to pay by American standards for a hotel room. And that was $30 a day. For a month that would have been $900—I would have already been $200 over. So I appealed to them at the hotel, and they allowed me the Russian rate, so it cost me $4 a day.

Once in Russia, how did you get into the hospitals?

Two days after I arrived I met Bill Worthy, the foreign correspondent in the Soviet Union for CBS News and the *Baltimore Afro-American*, and I told him my predicament. He said, "There's a party at the Romanian Embassy tomorrow night. Celebrating the 'liberation'—in quotation marks—of Romania." He had an invitation, he'd see if he could get me one. Well, he couldn't. He said, "Come on anyway," and I went with him. We were greeted by a bunch of KGB guys at the entrance. He showed his invitation, he slipped it back to me, and then I showed it, but they had also seen my passport. They saw the names were different. I ended up making a joke of the whole thing, and they waved me on. Within minutes I met the American ambassador and one of the top leaders of the Soviet Union, [Lazar Moiseyevich] Kaganovich. When he asked me what I was doing, I told him. He said, "Oh, we always think the *other* person is crazy!"

Later, one of the other guys came back to me and said, "Here's a phone number, the head of psychiatry. You're all set." And that's what gave me the entrée. I made this lovely little film; I was naïve enough to think that with a small camera you'd have sync sound and all that. It was a somewhat noisy camera. You couldn't even focus it. But I got what I needed.

What drew you to filmmaking?

I thought that if I were a writer I could tell what my experience was. I was not a writer, but I was a still photographer, so I suppose I extended that notion to the movie camera. I really did think there would be sync sound available, but that wasn't so. By necessity I had to narrate the film. I would rather not have. That issue became very important later on when I had suitable equipment, so we wouldn't need narration. That was a very big point that I've always made.

That the new lightweight, portable 16 mm equipment that came along a few years later liberated you?

Yes, and that you should come back with material good enough so that it holds its own story, rather than some Walter Cronkite giving you the message.

◀ **Albert and David Maysles on a motorcycle journey throughout Eastern Europe, 1957. "There were days that we traveled maybe 200 or 300 miles, and it was exhausting. But when the driver got too tired, he would retire to the rear seat, put his arms around the driver and hold his hands together. Then, as he was falling asleep, the driver would take a hand off the handle bar and clasp the two hands so they wouldn't fall apart. That's how we worked together."**

Photo courtesy of Maysles Films.

> *"The goal is to capture people with 'that magical combination of full truth and full subjectivity.'"*

Is your idea of an ideal documentary one without interviews?

Yes, ideally. But there are exceptions to that. There could be a great interview getting at something you wouldn't otherwise get, and getting it beautifully. But if you go into making a film with interviewing in mind, then you're foreclosing the opportunity to get something for real. One of the fundamental defects often found in interviewing is that the questions are rhetorical.

I'm reminded of the story that is told about Alice B. Toklas. She's with Gertrude Stein, who is dying, and Stein asks, "What is the answer?" When Toklas doesn't respond, Stein says, "In that case, what is the question?" In other words, the answer's already in the question.

I'll give you an example of how the interview mentality forecloses better opportunities. In *Salesman,* when Paul Brennan has had a rough day and he ends up in the cafeteria sitting at an empty table, just looking off into the blue, there wasn't anything we could have asked that could have made the scene more powerful than just his silence. Finally, he takes his leads, his cards, and raps them against the table, goes back to work.

Direct Cinema

What was the idea behind what came to be called "direct cinema" and how did it evolve?

Things really got moving upon meeting up with Robert Drew, Ricky Leacock, and D A Pennebaker. I think my brother David met Pennebaker first. At the end of '59, Leacock had already been working with Drew in the process of improving the equipment and conceptualizing an American form of cinema verité.

They were working technically on creating better equipment?

Technically, yes. But they were also developing in their own minds this different method of filming. In France it was called cinema verité. Pennebaker saw my film

Birth of a Genre

Prior to making his own films, Albert Maysles began his career as a cinematographer alongside fellow award-winning cameramen Richard Leacock, D A Pennebaker, and Robert Drew. Working together on many projects, they pioneered a type of filmmaking called *direct cinema*.

The invention of lighter, portable camera equipment allowed the filmmakers greater creative flexibility. Since they now could shoot with handheld cameras and record sync sound, this team of cameramen captured telling dramatic moments that did not require traditional news journalism techniques, such as voice-over narration and explanatory interviews. This new equipment also enabled a wave of political filmmaking that brought viewers inside places they would never have otherwise seen.

Free of the constraints of conventional nonfiction storytelling, the direct cinema approach allows events to unfold before the camera, much as they would if a film crew were not present. Maysles was one of the main cinematographers shooting Bob Drew's groundbreaking 1960s films *Primary* (a short film that follows the Kennedy-Humphrey presidential primary race) and *Yanki No!* (a film about anti-American viewpoints in Cuba and Latin America). That shooting style influenced both independent features and Hollywood filmmaking.

For cinematographers who embrace it, the direct cinema style (often conflated with cinema verité, the similar movement in France) radically alters how they approach their work. Such cinematographers are no longer in the service of a journalist's shot list, commissioned to capture facts on screen in a sequence that will be neatly explained to viewers by a reporter's voice. With direct cinema, cinematographers have much more pressure on them, since nothing is planned, artificially lit, or set up. The small crew shows up, and prepares to the best of its ability to capture the action as it occurs. Direct cinema cinematographers have more accountability, since during production they are actively collaborating with the director. Reality unfolds, and the role of the shooter is to seize the key moments without disturbing or affecting the events.

Maysles denies that the impetus behind the direct cinema movement was to capture events objectively. Instead, the goal as he sees it is to capture people with "that magical combination of full truth and full subjectivity."

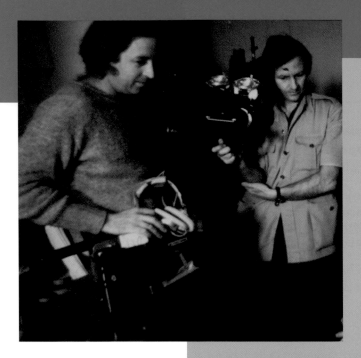

Shooting Maysles Style

Albert Maysles' shooting style was revolutionary within the filmmaking community; director Jean-Luc Godard called him "the best American cameraman." Maysles' style helped define the direct cinema approach, but without editors, he admits, there would be no story. When I asked him how he identified what was interesting from what he shot, he answered, "Now *that* you have to speak to the editor about. I don't get into that. I just make sure they've got the material for it. With *Salesman* and *Grey Gardens*, David supervised the editing, so he had that responsibility. But we also had very good editors."

Over the past five decades the Maysles brothers collaborated with many of the great documentary editors, including Charlotte Zwerin, Deborah Dixon, Bob Eisenhardt, and many others. They also helped foster the careers of some of the most successful producer/director teams working today: Bruce Sinofsky and Joe Berlinger; Muffie Meyers and Ellen Hovde; and numerous others.

"I was shooting something last night," Maysles tells me. "A friend of mine had an opening for her artwork, and there was another cameraperson with me who was not as experienced as myself. We were talking about shooting techniques. My camera has a manual zoom, so I can really use it very judiciously. When you're on something and then you move to something else, you should be using the zoom as you move. You need to open up a little wider, immediately, to exactly the right framing.

"For example, at this event in the gallery, there were a couple of dancers from India, and a violinist sitting on a chair, and over here were all these people gathering around. So I would go back and forth between the dancers, the violinist, and the audience. But when it came time to frame the movement, I found myself ending up with a perfectly composed shot. It was almost like a miracle! Now, I had to be composing it as I was zooming in, but it worked just beautifully."

Albert and David Maysles during the shooting of *Gimme Shelter*. In a February 2000 interview with Anne Lewis of *The Austin Chronicle*, Albert Maysles explained how trust is communicated in the day-to-day filmmaking experience, "The cameraman has to have what I call 'the gaze'—empathy—the way you look at the people you're shooting and how you establish their trust. Paying attention to people is an extremely powerful force of recognition and of love: that's documentary at its best. Without their trust, you're just a walking zombie with a camera and your subjects don't connect.'"

Photo courtesy of Maysles Films.

What about—dare I say the word?—objectivity?

Almost any time I've talked about documentaries, this thing comes up: Can you be subjective and objective? I think the thing that bridges the gap is the love and respect you give to the people and events that you're filming. You want to be without prejudice, have an open mind, a loving spirit, a talent for gaining access to people, maintaining a rapport with them, a confidence that you really belong there based on a true feeling of doing the right thing for them, for yourself, for the film—all that allows you to express emotions that really get to the heart of another person—and without the cold objectivity of a scientific report.

I think one thing that may help a lot in that regard is that I was studying to be a social scientist. I also had this confidence as an artist with a camera. With the objectivity of a scientist combined with the heart of a lover of humanity, I could be faithful to both the emotional side and the factual.

Two truths.

Yes, there's room for both. There was a magazine article with a discussion of two things: social issue films and political issue films. I called up the editor and I said, it was a terrific piece. But there's another kind too—the nonissue film.

How can any documentary avoid raising questions? What do you mean by a "nonissue film"?

Well, it's not that you're trying to avoid issues, but the films that are called political or social issue films are advocacy films. And once you begin to advocate, then you're taking sides. You're getting into propaganda, and that's a dangerous route.

Primary

Can you give me an example of when you've resisted the expression of your own point of view?

It's funny. Actually, with *Primary* many people have told me, "Gee, you really had it in for Humphrey." But in fact, all of us who made the film—there was a whole group of us—if you asked us whom we wanted to win, we were for Humphrey.

Why do you think the film gives the opposite impression?

Because people were so taken in by Kennedy's eliteness and his charisma, that by comparison they think that Humphrey looks like a farm boy or something.

Image does him in.

Yeah. But if you examine his record in the Senate, Humphrey had a fantastic record. From that standpoint, and his connection with the common man, you could argue very well that he might be the better man. So we weren't [encouraging support for] one or the other, but how do you control the prejudices of the public?

One of the legendary shots in *Primary* is that great high-angle one of Kennedy walking into the auditorium. I believe that's yours.

That was my first time with a camera that had sync sound. That shot was Pennebaker's idea. He's the one that suggested that I might follow Kennedy into this auditorium holding the camera above. He supplied me with an extremely wide-angle 5.7 mm lens, which was very unusual. In those days, no one was using a lens like that, because they'd think it was too distorted. But I knew, as Penne did, too, that I could capture this piece of psychology, with the back of Kennedy's head in the middle of the frame. The camera had to be high enough so that it was just above Kennedy's head, so you could be looking into the faces of people that he was meeting as he was walking along. You got exactly *his* point of view, which, of course, you never see on the news.

Yanki No!

You worked on several films after *Primary*. One, *Yanki No!* released in 1960 and directed by Robert Drew, included footage you shot in Cuba. How did you make contact with Castro and persuade him to let you film him?

It's a funny story. I go to Cuba not knowing anything more about Cuba than anybody else, and having no contacts. Get off the plane, jump into a cab, turn to the cabdriver and say, "Where's Fidel?" In those days people knew where he was, just ordinary people. The cabdriver said, "Oh, he's addressing a large group of women at this auditorium." So I said, "Well, take me there."

At the auditorium, I get as close as I can to him, which is not very close— maybe 20, 25 feet. But I want to get closer to him, so I stick a 200 mm lens on the camera, which is quite a telephoto lens, which would bring me so close that I'd be just a little bit within his face. And as I'm raising the camera to my shoulder, and as he's giving this eloquent, powerful speech, he happens to turn in my direction and we connect eyeballs. And that's great, because I could tell that it was OK. I put it on my shoulder and got the most fantastic shot, taking advantage of what might otherwise be a disadvantage. I couldn't hold it steady as a rock, and I don't like these steady-as-a-rock shots. Steady, but not mechanically steady.

Then somehow I got in with him. There were a couple of days that I was with Fidel around the clock. There was one day, I remember, it was 3 o'clock in the morning and he says, "Let's get something to eat." So we go to a restaurant. Of course, Fidel doesn't just sit down and order a meal from the menu. He goes to the kitchen and orders what he wants. As he put his order in, he looks around the kitchen and sees a telephone on the wall. He picks up the telephone, slips through the doorway—I guess to have some privacy, but he's talking loud enough so I could hear everything he's saying and I'm recording it. Without his presence there was, nevertheless, the telephone cable hanging loose at times, stretched and going back. It was so graphic—a polygraph recording of his psychodynamics. The only thing that had me concerned was that I was hoping the camera wouldn't run out so I could carry all the way through to the point where he would come out. And it did. I had him finishing his talk and hanging up at the very end. Beautiful shot.

Why did you want to go to Cuba in the first place?

I guess the same instinct that brought me to Russia, it was a place where it's difficult to get to. When I went to Russia the whole idea was to, at long last, see what Russians look like, humanize them. Someone should humanize Iraqis right now. We don't have a human perspective.

Salesman

Salesman **follows four door-to-door Bible peddlers, but mainly focuses on one, Paul Brennan, an Irishman from Boston. Describe** *Salesman*.

It shows all of us what life is for many of us. I think you could say that it was the first nonfiction feature film. The parallel was Truman Capote's *In Cold Blood,* which was the first nonfiction novel. With *Salesman*, you could make a film that would just tear those people apart. Even Paul, when he misbehaves, he's like the rest of them: pushing a product on people.

As cinematographer, you're concerned with how the shot composition positions the film viewer in relationship to the subjects being filmed.

The way I work is as one would *see* it—only with a more acute eye. One thing that I hate, which is so much the custom in cinematography, is that the subject be on one side of the screen; that's not the way you see people. It's wrong because it's so artificial. As a viewer, and as a photographer, you want to get as close as possible to that person, to their feelings, and to what the person has to say. To shove that person to the side makes for something fashionable but, I would say, improper.

With *Salesman***, I understand that you had a personal connection to the subject.**

My brother and I suffered a great deal of anti-Semitism in Boston at the hands of the Irish. Paul and all of those guys are Irishmen. So it was our opportunity to make amends for the cultural division. I mean, those guys remained our great

◀ Paul Brennan of *Salesman*, a theatrically released documentary that was selected by the Library of Congress as one of the best American films ever made.

Photo courtesy of Maysles Films.

▼ Albert and David Maysles filming *Salesman*. David Denby's 1969 review of *Salesman* reveals the relative newness of direct cinema documentaries, and how seductive the fly-on-the-wall style can be. Denby writes, "Movie purists may object to some of the techniques employed by the Maysles brothers. They have eliminated from the film all evidence that the people being photographed—the salesmen and their customers—are aware of the presence of the camera."

Phto courtesy of Maysles Films.

The five directors of *Grey Gardens*, from top left, David Maysles, Muffie Meyers, Albert Maysles, Ellen Hovde, and Susan Froemke.

Photo courtesy of Marianne Barcellona © 2005.

You told me earlier that after a few weeks of shooting Radziwill's original concept, you met to screen the dailies. How did it become clear to you that you should focus on the Beales?

We sat right here in this room and projected the stuff for Lee, and we could see that the real story was the Beales, and it was so powerful that it was upstaging her stuff. There was an ongoing story, an ongoing *relationship* that was so profound. We didn't have to construct anything; there was always something going on. Several months later we took on the story of the Beales as a full-time film for ourselves.

So right away, it became a mother-daughter story?

I think we realized well into the editing, or maybe even more so after the film was completed, that we were dealing with the most profound human relationship: the mother-daughter relationship. It's so interesting when you consider that in making a documentary, to go at it really well, it's a process of discovery.

"In making a documentary, to go at it really well, it's a process of discovery."

Even when the film was finished we hadn't quite recognized that we had a treasure house of information about the mother-daughter relationship. I think that it would have been an eye opener even for Freud. Because he was fascinated with the Oedipal complex, the mother-son relationship, even in his studies and beyond, people hadn't really given much attention to this other relationship, which is even more profound. *Grey Gardens* was a discovery of that, an explanation of it, and an elucidation of it.

Christo

Over the past three decades, you've collaborated with public space artists Christo and Jeanne-Claude on five—soon to be six—films. Tell me how the first film project came to be.

In 1962, we were showing our first film, *Showmen*, in Paris, and a friend there said, "The Christos would like to see the film." So he invites the Christos. And sure enough, they see the film and we're instant soul mates, because they could see us filming one of their projects. And we could see, from what they told us of their projects, it was no longer just an artist standing by an easel. The projects are an integral part of real life that's going on, the kind of thing that we're always looking for. It wasn't so long—I guess it was ten years or so—before a project came along, the Valley Curtain. *Christo's Valley Curtain* was the first film we made of his work. Then it went on from there. Four more projects (*Running Fence, Islands, Umbrellas, Christo in Paris*).

You met Christo and Jeanne-Claude, and ten years later you start to shoot.

That's right.

▶ **From *Christo's Valley Curtain*, the first of a six film series on the artwork of Christo and Jeanne-Claude, produced by Albert and David Maysles.**

Photos courtesy of Christo and Jeanne-Claude.

▼ **From *Islands*. Left, the public space artist Christo drafts plans for his installation. Right, the installation art piece, *Islands*.**

Photos courtesy of Christo and Jeanne-Claude.

How different are those films from other Maysles films?

It's still the same thing. In so many of these Christo projects he's got to fight to get permission to do them, and so that's a whole drama—the politics of it, the economics of it, the social stuff. Then, as with each documentary, whether it's a Christo project or not, there's some unexpected elements. For example, I arranged a meeting with Joan Mondale, who is very into art. She came to this room, and she saw *Running Fence*, and she said, "We've got to get this film in every American embassy around the world, because it tells so much about how a democracy works." We thought about that. She was right.

How so?

All those 17 or so meetings where people liked the idea of the project or didn't like it, and the board members who had to decide on whether to give permission to construct the fence, right? And the debate, and the pros and cons, and then, finally, they have to practically break the law—or maybe they do, I don't know—and they get it done.

For those who haven't seen it, would you describe *Running Fence*?

It was a fence made of white fabric that was 18 feet high and 24 miles long. It started in the water of the Pacific, running up the hillside into one hill and valley after another, going east across California [in

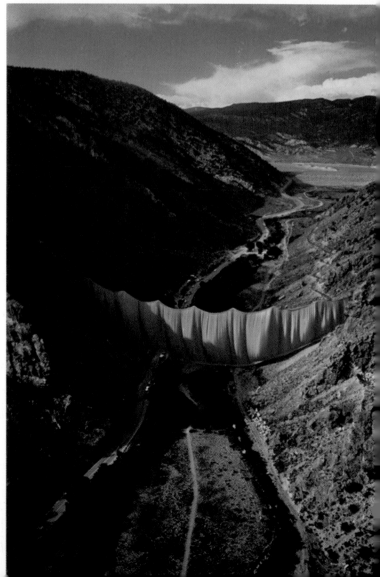

Marin and Sonoma counties, just north of San Francisco]. I've always thought of some of his projects, which are wrappings or, in this case, a fence, as drawing their inspiration from his own experiences behind the Iron Curtain. So this was a white curtain that, as fences do, it should cut off communication from one side to the other. But being a work of art, and being only made of fabric, it comes to be just the opposite. It brings people together. It brings them together physically. I think something like a million people saw it. It brings them together to think about what art is all about, and to question whether, indeed, this *is* a work of art. What is art anyway? And also, people have to consider what their priorities are. Would it have been better somehow for the people to have spent those millions of dollars on hospitals? People have a much lower regard for art than for social care. And does one have to exclude the other? That came up. Those were some of the things that were provoked by the project itself.

Umbrellas was unique in that it was located in two countries.

Yes, it was international. It was created in two countries. Yellow umbrellas in California and blue ones in Japan. When you look at those pictures, how could he ever afford it, how could he ever have done it? How could those hills and valleys be any more beautiful than what nature had bestowed? That's a question that comes up too, perhaps, at least in my mind, for the Gates project [in New York's Central Park]. How can such a beautiful park be enhanced by a work of human beings?

Lighting and the Move to Video

What's your approach to lighting?

The well lit shot uses no artificial lights, no lights of your own. Right now, the well lit shot would be what you and I look like right now. When we did *Salesman* we had film that wasn't as sensitive to light as now, so we had to add light. So we'd carry with us a little stand and a light source and we just bounced light off the ceiling. We would have preferred no lights, but we needed it in that case. It was

Documentaries—Watching and Making

For Maysles, to watch a compelling documentary film is to become "engaged in a process that is so human and so lacking, especially in our sophisticated societies." He feels that the Iraq war "never would have happened if we had a few films of Iraqi people. It wouldn't be going on now the way it is without more skepticism if we were looking at what's happened there. We haven't even seen a photograph of what Baghdad looks like from the air having been bombed to hell. Have you? I haven't seen it. That's about the first basic—they bombed Baghdad, let's take a look at it. But, from there we can get into people's *lives*."

Of documentary filmmaking, Maysles says, "I can't think of a better profession and it's not just because I earn a living by it. Although, I don't know—do I earn a living by it?" he laughs, gesturing around at his spare midtown offices. "It's not just that. It's that I'm doing good all the way around. I'm making a film that I can be proud of. I'm doing a service, the ultimate service, for people that I'm filming, giving them recognition and paying attention to them, not as they would be or should be or shouldn't be, but who they *are*. That's what people need, right? And then, there's the benefit to the audience: Millions of people can step into the lives of people they never otherwise would have met, and learn something.

How did you conceive of this project?

I love to meet people on trains and buses, and I think no matter where I meet somebody it's easy for me to gain access to them. But there's a special ambience on a train, where that process is easier. So I thought it'd be interesting to film people I meet on trains. Some of what happens on the train as they talk to me, or are in conversation with someone else, would be in the film, but most of what I'm after is the story that pops up when they're on the train—something suggesting what might happen when they get off the train. I'm getting into new territory in the genres of documentary. This would be parallel to the short-story collection in literature because it would be made up of half a dozen or so short stories connected to the train.

But nonfiction.

Totally nonfiction. I want these short stories to be so strong, that if Tolstoy or Borges saw one of them they'd say, "Oh my goodness, I've got to put down my pen and pencil and pick up a camera." The strongest story I've run across so far—I've really just begun—is a story that I discovered as I was making an early research trip, so I didn't have a camera with me. If I shot it I'd still want to know that it wouldn't hurt the woman I was filming, but it gives you an idea of how powerful a story one can get. The train was on its way across the country. We had stopped in a station. I looked out the window and saw a group of three people—a couple and a woman. They're very happy. Why, I don't know, because I can't hear their conversation. After the train left the station, I walked through the train and I came across that third person. She was sitting alone, crying. I joined her, and the first thing she said was, "I still can't make up my mind." Then she told me that she's married to a man who changes his jobs and sometimes it means leaving where her family and friends are and moving on to another place. She was joining her husband at a new house that they just bought together. Then she went back to crying, and said, "I still can't make up my mind, because the couple I left behind, he's the one I really love." It's all there, just waiting. Just waiting.

"It's all there, just waiting. Just waiting."

Because these stories are totally random, we're getting a mix that includes happy stories, which would almost never occur on television, because the assumption is that a happy story isn't dramatic.

Editing

Finding the Film

"I'm very particular about the kind of cuts I make," says veteran documentary editor Geof Bartz, "because good cutting is indistinguishable from good structure." Indeed, the sign of great film editing, most agree, is when the audience fails to notice the cutting at all. Bartz, like all the editors I spoke with, considers creating absorbing narrative that puts the viewer inside of the story by delivering entertaining scenes and substance to be at the heart of his search to find the film.

The documentary editor is like a sculptor whose materials are restricted to found artifacts of media: photographs, professionally shot footage, archival material, home movies, interviews, music, and transcripts. Today's editors working in the digital realm also have animation, graphics, and effects at their disposal to construct a cinematic story line. But while the equipment used to edit documentaries evolves at an ever-accelerating pace—from a Steenbeck, Moviola, or reel-to-reel video editing system of ten years ago to your average personal computer today—the craft of storytelling remains at the core of editors' work. Editor Larry Silk says, "Every cut is a disturbance of reality, so the trick is to cut artfully so the cut *gives* you more than the disturbance it creates." Documentary editing ties together seemingly mundane moments that may lack inherent drama in a way that moves the plot forward, creates intrigue, portrays an engrossing reality, and brings the larger significance of the events to the surface of the film.

In editing, one advocates for the audience. While most audiences do not recognize what the process of editing entails, the editor's dedication to the audience can be the strongest within the crew. Independent film editor and NYU film school associate professor Carol Dysinger explains, "Anybody can make a movie make sense, but can you make the movie and make sure that all the bits of truth and life that they managed to capture—you can't save them all, but the little moments, the best stuff—is it in there? For a documentary editor, that's key. There are so many times that people will say, 'Well, that doesn't really fit. That should go.' And I'm saying, 'No, that's the only good thing on the *screen!* If it doesn't fit, the rest of it should go and we'll figure out another way.' You have to sustain a commitment to what's alive for an audience."

As Silk describes it, "Editors are always thinking audience; we're the proxy for the audience. We love our audience, and we want them to stick with it, but I'm trying to give the audience the experience of what's happening in a way that you would *want* to perceive it—approximating the experience of being there, but using the dramatic excitement. That's why they're buying the film in the first place." Bartz says that the loyalty an editor feels is because the editor is the audience's "surrogate": the only one who possesses the privilege to improve the film. "At the end of the day, I'll sit back and say, 'Is this something I would *want* to watch?' And if there's something I don't like, I'll work on that, because I'm the audience member who actually gets to change this film."

As the guardian of entertainment values, the editor asks of each film: What is this really *about?* Or, as Dysinger asks: "How are you going to look at it differently at the beginning than at the end?"

> *"Stories may indeed be told without editing… but in an important way the beginning of editing is the beginning of cinema itself."*
>
> —*Mark Le Fanu*

Every editor I interviewed spoke of the importance of emotional intuition. They ask: What does the audience know emotionally at the end of the film that they did not know before? The literal events documented in the film need to build towards larger themes. Successful editing makes clear in the subtext that the specific experiences portrayed in the film imply larger consequences. Steve James's and Peter Gilbert's *Hoop Dreams*, a hit at Sundance and in theaters, received such a strong response not only due to the candid moments it recorded, but because of the gravity of the social problems it diagnosed, stirring a national debate over the decaying inner city educational system, the role of parents in governing teenage career paths, and ethical responsibility in sports recruiting.

While editing *Deadline,* the Sundance Film Festival hit that premiered on NBC, Dysinger describes her and the two directors' discovery of the film's intention. "When we found the speech where Gov. George Ryan said the Lincoln line—that mercy bears greater fruits than strict justice, and by the grace of God may this be so—I thought, 'That's the whole movie: how scary mercy is.' It's *scary,* because you don't know what they're going to do. So, to me, that was what gave me the clue: 'I need to get the audience to that line, I need to make them *feel* that thought.'" Finding the larger concerns a documentary raises and weaving them invisibly into a compelling storyline are the rare accomplishments of a great editor.

But not every documentary seeks to call attention to social inequities. In *Punk,* a series about the history of punk music, Dysinger sought out the film's essential theme, again, by poring through material, listening, and thoughtfully respond- ing. "There was an interview with Pete Townshend, who lost a lot of friends. He said something like, 'You think rock 'n' roll is this fire, this beautiful fire, but you get close to the beautiful lovely fire and you realize what it's burning is bodies.' I found that and felt, 'This is it. It's beautiful—but it's caustic.' It's the same thing you do with a script. It's finding the *paradox* that you want to explore both sides of. Something is interesting because it is paradoxical." Given no script and vague bearings, the documentary editor must hunt carefully through the material, seek- ing any indication of what the footage communicates on emotional, intellectual, and structural levels.

How an editor identifies those telling moments, or manipulates the sequential structure so that they *appear* telling, is where the craft, the intricacy, and the fun enter in. Some accomplish plot construction through endless screening, rescreen- ing, experimentation, introspection, and deliberation. Others rely on proven techniques of juxtaposition, or by cutting "B roll" (visual material shot with the intention that audio from another source will be paired with it) to the related voice-over of an interview, which—depending on the connotation of the combined footage—may result in one of many dramatic effects.

Undeniably, documentary editors have a challenging job. They are often left alone in a room full of loosely related material and asked to "find the story," as if the task were as simple as a game of hide-and-go-seek. "You always focus on what you know," editor Paula Heredia says, "because you always have a very large list of things that you don't know." In many cases, the editor is ultimately responsible for delivering the final film: pacing the scenes, structuring the story line, concealing the limitations of the material. As Silk describes it, "I'm helpless, for the most part. I'm dealing with what I've got. So I have to figure out what I can do with what I've got. And every artist has to deal with what the parameters forced on them are imposing. How much money? How much time? How much backing? What are the physical creative limitations they suffer? What are the parameters of the struggle that every artist is dealing with? Like Michelangelo on his back doing the Sistine Chapel; I'm sure his back was one of his limitations."

Geof
Bartz

Editor

Crafting
Cinematic Television

GEOF BARTZ, WHO HAS WORKED IN THE FILM INDUSTRY FOR OVER 30 years, has received two Academy Awards for his film editing. Before he joined HBO's staff, Bartz's documentary editing credits included many of the cult classics—such as *Pumping Iron* and *Stripper*—that nontraditional documentary viewers watch repeatedly. "To me, the whole challenge of editing is to try to get people inside of a story," Bartz says, "I'm very devoted to storytelling." Not coincidentally, he started out as a cinephile and an audience member. In college he majored in biology, but joined a film society as an undergraduate. "We'd get together and watch these great, original films that you couldn't see anywhere else. I saw the rushes of *Gunsmoke*, and first came across the idea that there is a scene that's played, and then replayed three different times, cut different ways by different editors. It was like the scales fell off my eyes: It didn't come out of the camera that way! Somebody made decisions to link those shots that way." This was a different way of experimenting, and Bartz knew he wanted to become a film editor.

Geof Bartz filmography

Bartz attended film school at Columbia University with many of the leading producers and editors working in filmmaking today. Later, he taught film editing in the graduate division at Columbia, using the same rushes that originally inspired him. "I give the rushes to my students to cut their own way. I've probably seen those scenes cut 300 different ways. And they are all different—it's different every time. Some of them are really very good! And some of them are pretty bad—but the idea is that there's this experimentation that's possible with editing film that is not possible with any other medium. I'm fascinated by that."

As an educator, Bartz developed a rare talent for communicating what is to many an indecipherable art form: the craft of documentary editing. His own work has been for great producers such as David Grubin (*The American Experience: LBJ, FDR, TR, Truman,* and *America: 1900*) and Albert Maysles. He describes his editing style as "not flashy," but he devotes his attention to meticulous story structure and "good cutting." His concern, first and foremost, is with entertaining the audience by drawing them into the narrative through character development. To that end, he fights to limit the amount of exposition needed to tell the story, and often advocates for limited narration or title cards—referencing the style of original verité filmmakers, but with a contemporary flair.

Today, Bartz uses his aptitude for verbalizing cinematic concepts to work with both seasoned and novice filmmakers as supervising editor for HBO, where he has edited or consulted on dozens of award-winning films, often as the unsung hero of the project. As president of HBO Documentary Sheila Nevins relates the story, "I met Geof as an admirer, his credit rolling by on a screen, I didn't meet him as an employer. I guess I'm still an admirer. Or, I should say, a worshipper. I saw some show about the brain… then I'd also seen *Pumping Iron*, and I had recognized the same spelling of that name. I thought that both of those were very brilliantly assembled."

Nevins was buying more documentaries made by independent filmmakers, and she hired Bartz as HBO's "resident physician." A staff arrangement as supervising editor for documentary programming at a network as prolific and prestigious as HBO is a unique position in the documentary editing field, as most long-form projects are cut by freelance editors who are hired by independent producers. Hence, Bartz holds a coveted position among editors. For him, it is an opportunity to work in an uncensored, advertising-free environment, where "you can really show real stuff: violence, sex, everything." Nevins describes the job as "inseparable from the success of what we do, and the remaking of the either completed or the needing-to-be-remedied documentary that we might acquire. The filmmakers tend to love him, and they love their film being repaired and twisted about and thrown up in the air and coming down again with the pieces in a different order. It's just been a great collaboration and a great gift to HBO to have him here."

Geof Bartz at work in the edit room.

Photo courtesy of Geof Bartz.

· · ·

All the editors I've spoken with have discussed the difference between cutting a feature film, in which one works with takes and a script, and cutting a documentary, in which editors discover the story in the footage—in some cases arbitrarily, or independent of the director. Many documentary editors liken this process to scriptwriting. Do you?

Absolutely. When I taught film editing at Columbia University, I used to tell my students that the challenge for fiction film editors was making *fake* people—otherwise known as actors—believable inside of a ready-made story provided by

In 1999, Geof Bartz and Robert B. Weide shared an Emmy for editing *Lenny Bruce: Swear to Tell the Truth*.

Photo by Craig T. Mathew, courtesy of Geof Bartz.

a scriptwriter, while documentary editors had *real* people but were challenged to find a dramatic story—or at least a compelling structure—somewhere, somehow in the hundreds of hours of footage that is dumped in their laps.

Now it's true that scriptwriters can go anywhere they want in their heads to solve a story problem while documentary editors are limited to the footage a producer brings to the cutting room. But both must use their imaginations to draw an audience into a story that has a beginning, a middle, and an end—or to find a structure that may not be a traditional story but that, nevertheless, builds to a satisfying conclusion.

Tell me about your role as supervising editor at HBO.

One of the goals of HBO is we want to create something different than what you can get for free on NBC. Sheila Nevins wants to keep people paying their $30 or $40 a month. So what the magazine shows deliver as headlines stated up front, we try to bury in dramatic storytelling. There are three ways in which films come to me at HBO. Sometimes they're just dailies. Other times there's a film we've acquired, and it's in progress, in which case I need to work with the director and maybe another editor on making it fit within HBO's format. And then there's the third kind: consulting, where I don't do any of the hands-on editing.

You enjoy the diverse roles you play.

I do. We work with filmmakers who often have very little money, but an enormous amount of passion. It's important to embrace them, and let them champion their story—because they are often the film's greatest asset.

Exposition and Eliminating Redundancies

Where do you begin, when you work with a filmmaker who is new to HBO and their film succeeded on the festival circuit, but HBO feels it needs "medicating?"

Well, *entertaining* is a dirty word for some people, but to me it's what you should be focusing on as an editor. Focus on cutting out all the boring stuff, all the information that gets repeated again and again. Sometimes as a director you don't even know that you're being redundant—but I always look to the next scene to tell me something new. If it's information, or an emotion that you've already felt, show them something else.

When you first start working with them, many documentary filmmakers are not concerned with making an entertaining film?

One of the most common mistakes filmmakers make is they get caught up in how you reveal the exposition. People often begin a film with all these facts, all this background on the characters or on the subject—information that you think the audience needs to know. What you want to try to do is let the story unfold—start with something weird or surprising or wacky or mysterious. There are different philosophies on what that first scene should be; some people like to start with a straight-cut interview. I rarely do that—but sometimes it works. If you do start with a talking head, then at least start at a really unusual point in the interview, to arouse the audience's curiosity.

Documentary filmmakers often feel they need to explain the issue, which gets in the way of cinematic storytelling. But how do you determine what the audience needs to know, and what should be allowed to be discovered through the footage?

Sometimes you do have to start the film with a few facts. Like we just took a film that was edited in Poland, and we cut it slightly here. It was called *The Children of Leningradsky*, about homeless children who lived in subway stations in Moscow. There were about 30,000 of them. But the film that we got didn't have any big idea at the head of it. You weren't sure: Are you just watching the lives of twleve kids who happen to live in subway stations, or is this just a little slice of life? We did put a title card, a fact, at the head of that film: "In the former Soviet Union there are 3 million homeless children, children without their parents; 30,000 in Moscow, many in the subway stations." So all of a sudden you give a context to this story and hope that they'll take it as not just a little slice of life, but a slice of a much larger piece of life.

You're orienting viewers, setting up the scope of the problem so that when you introduce specific characters that bring the story to life, their stories have more weight.

Yes. Another example is, I worked with a filmmaker [Cynthia Wade] on the initial cut called *Shelter Dogs*, about dogs in shelters. When I first heard about that film I

Two of the stars of *Shelter Dogs*. "To me, the whole challenge of editing is to try to get people *inside* of a story."

Photo by Heidi Gutman, courtesy of director Cynthia Wade.

▶ Sue Sternberg has dedicated her life to animal rescue. "When I first heard about that film," says Bartz, "I thought, 'It's a nice little story about a woman who loves dogs.' But it's a far more complicated, nuanced film."

Photos by Heidi Gutman, courtesy of director Cynthia Wade.

thought, "It's a nice little story about a woman who loves dogs." But it's a far more complicated, nuanced film. There are millions of dogs who end up in shelters every year. So what do you do? Are they safe enough to put into homes, where there are children? Should you destroy some of them, or keep them locked away in cages for their entire lives? There are philosophical and moral problems there that make it a complex story with twists and turns. It's a story that goes beyond what you expect this film to be about.

Once again, we started with this fact that there are millions of them every year in the shelters of the United States. So there's a huge problem. And in her first cut she had taken all the information that she had about the main character and pumped it into the first scene. Everything there was to know about this character: her philosophy, where she grew up, why she does this, how the shelter worked, all this stuff. And what happened is that the viewer was inundated with a bunch of information, not pulled into the story. So in the recutting of it we decided we would parse out these facts. What's something you might need to know at the very beginning? The number of dogs that are affected by this problem. Then we had to figure out how long can the story go where you just see her working with the animals, working with people who drop off animals, putting animals in cages, and wondering whether or not they're going to be adopted. Then, it can come to a piece of information; such as where does she come from and why does she do it? If you do that, if you pull that off, people are going to listen to the why and the wherefore—but if they haven't seen her actions, they don't really care about her. They're not drawn into a story. To me, the whole challenge of editing is to try to get people *inside* of a story.

How do you do that—put the viewer inside of a story?

The way I really like to think about it is to get them to step onto a boat that's going down a river, which just allows them to be carried along the river. But along the river there are going to be some landmarks, and some signs along the way, that are going to tell you a little bit about this river. You'll be drawn along, you'll be drawn into the story. I think you *need* the story. That's why people go to movies, they want to be drawn inside the stories.

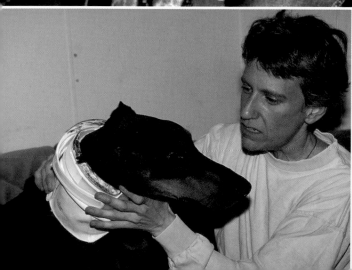

COME IN AND ADOPT A DOG or CAT

Bending the Rules of Cinema Verité

In your boat metaphor, what do the landmarks represent—information that bridges the gap between scenes?

Yes, the landmarks I'm talking about are pieces of exposition. Like, where do the characters come from, why do they do it, when were they born? In a magazine article you always see that: There's always a big preamble before you get into the story. In *Pumping Iron* it's a long time, at least 15 or 20 minutes, before you get the backstory of Arnold Schwarzenegger. So you were immersed in the world of body-building. But we were faced with a bit of a dilemma with that film, because in 1975 or '76, when we were cutting the film, it was the height of cinema verité. And the rules, the so-called "rules of cinema verité," were that you really should only use the sync dailies. There should be no narration, no music, no interviews, no talking heads, no voice-over from the characters in the film. In the Frederick Wiseman form, the film is carved out only from the dailies. I don't mean there's not a lot of editing going on, but those devices that I mentioned, which were standard devices that editors use, supposedly you were not supposed to use those. It's a little bit like—what's that movement now, the European movement?

Dogma '95?

Right. It was the Dogma '95 of its day.

When I spoke with Albert Maysles, he shared with me his own "Rules for Direct Cinema."

Well, he was one of the guys who invented the rules! But when we started to cut *Pumping Iron* that way, it was an interesting film to watch, because it's interesting to watch people do what they're doing. But I know they [director George Butler and producer Jerome Gary] wanted this thing to be *fun* for people to watch. They wanted people to go to the movies. And we felt, honestly, that people didn't watch cinema verité to have fun.

Why *did* they watch cinema verité?

They watched it as an exercise in a type of pure filmmaking, which was fascinating, but it didn't draw in a very large audience. So with *Pumping Iron* we said, this is *mostly* going to be verité style, but we are going to bring in some external elements, primarily music. And there were these interesting interviews from Arnold. You couldn't *not* have them, because otherwise you really miss out on a lot. And we found out also you needed a little bit of—God forbid, this was supposed to be the worst possible thing to have in verité—narration, just to orient people as to where they were, and what exactly was bodybuilding. I think, today, honestly, people would do it with title cards rather than with a voice-over. But then our solution was to use Charles Gaines, who was the writer. He wrote a little bit of narration, and that was parsed out along the way as it was needed.

*"**Entertaining** is a dirty word for some people, but to me it's what you should be focusing on as an editor."*

Photo courtesy of Pumping Iron America, Inc.

***Pumping Iron* was shot verité style—observationally—but as you edited it with Larry Silk, you brought in music, interviews, and voice-over. Was that heretical?**

Not really. To tell you the truth, all these debates are kind of within the film community. And outside the film community, and even within the film community, it's not like people are sitting around the salons talking about this stuff. It's kind of in the air.

Were Gary and Butler disappointed that it could not be pulled off in a pure verité style?

Well, from that moment to the end of the film had to be a very short time, because everything else after that was going to be anticlimactic. That was the heart of the story. That was the resolution of the conflict. And either you got rid of everything else or you had to find a way—which we ultimately did—to take everything that followed that point, and cheat it into the beginning of the film as if it happened before. But it couldn't happen after that moment.

I don't know whether that's a good example or not, but it's always stuck in my mind. You can usually see where the end of the story should be, and then everything else can be used to build to that moment. Whether it happened in real time afterwards, or it happened before, it was all meant to build to that moment.

At what point do you start looking at structure in terms of a time line? Do you begin with that? When you work with filmmakers, do you start to talk to them in the beginning about what they've shot, and where they feel the critical moments are, or do wait until you screen their footage?

In the ideal world, you screen the dailies with the director, and you talk in a very loose way. Then the editor makes selects, and boils down the dailies to about 30 percent of that material. That is really important to do when you're starting out. I've gotten to the point now where I get around that, but when you're starting out it's important not to try to tackle everything, but to tackle a small amount of it—and I mean less than half. Get it down. It's boring because you're not making a movie at that point, you're just carving out stuff that's interesting.

What do you look for when you're making selects?

Anything that has some interesting moments in it. As you're screening, you say, "Here's another moment that's interesting. This is boring. This is a shot that may be useful because it's the exterior of a building and maybe I need the exterior of a building." You just find little things that are useful. You organize it in a way that you can find it easily—by character, by topic, by time period, whatever you want, as long as you can figure out how to get to that stuff easily. Then you watch that 30 percent with the director, and things begin to resonate that didn't resonate in the dailies. I'm not sure why that is. I guess that's like if you have a big forest and you cut down a bunch of trees, you can begin to see, oh, these are the good trees, you know? That one's a *really* good tree. I'm going to keep that in the landscape. It's still not telling you the exact order that the trees are supposed to go in, but maybe it's already been very clear from the dailies where the film's going to go. Or maybe you discovered it in that process.

So the structuring of the film comes together at different times. There's no formula.

There's no formula. I hate to cop out, but a lot of it is just intuition. But then someone once said to me, "What you call intuition really is just a bunch of experience. You've been doing this a long time, so you think it's intuition. It wasn't intuition when you were starting out." And they're absolutely right. What *feels* like intuition to people who have been doing this for a long time is insight gained from a lot of accumulated mistakes. I think that's really what intuition is: a lot of experience. But I think you do have to be somewhat in touch with—I hate to say it—in touch with feelings. Not *your* feelings, but just feelings in general, because that's really what you're working with. How you line that stuff up—what makes a good beginning and what makes a good end, and what it's all supposed to mean— that is a long, long hard road most of the time; sometimes it's several years. You hear about these films, like *Grey Gardens*, it took two years to edit.

A Cool Eye: Editorial Distance

When beginning to edit a long-form documentary project, the first challenge involves winnowing down the material—which can be hundreds of hours—prior to having a full grasp of what the ultimate story line will become. Bartz works closely with HBO's filmmakers—who often come to HBO after independently beginning to shoot a project—and with President of HBO Documentary / Executive Producer Sheila Nevins to determine the story's structure. Nevins says she often works alongside the postproduction team as "the cool eye in an editing room sometimes for days, sometimes for hours, sometimes for nights. Because, in fact, I'm the one who usually wasn't in the field, so I see the product the way the audience sees the product, and I am working for that audience."

In 2001, Bartz edited *Dwarfs: Not a Fairy Tale* for HBO. As an editor, with each film, Bartz must determine what he has to work with—which in this case was the quality of footage, the fortitude and ordinariness of the characters, and the commitment of the filmmaker. When the project came to him, filmmaker Lisa Hedley had started with seven separate stories of different dwarfs' daily life experiences. Bartz was tasked with giving the project structure to integrate the story lines, and create a compelling plot.

Bartz explains, "First, I suggested we cut it down from seven to five stories," in order to avoid redundancy. "So you have one story that has a happy ending—that's a must! And then you have another story that has a tragic ending. In one, there is a man who becomes a famous surgeon ... only he's small. And in another you have a woman who is tired of being little, so she has an operation to lengthen herself." The next challenge was to develop an order that would draw in an audience, by portraying the characters' stories in a gripping way. Bartz says, "We started out with the sad ending. We certainly didn't want to *end* with the sad ending!" From there, the chronology came together by following an emotional through-line. Bartz adds, "The woman who was making it had a daughter who was small, so she wanted the film to be moving," to be humanistic, for audiences to identify with the characters as they would other people.

What do you do when you are stuck, when you hit a roadblock?

One of the classic techniques is just going away. Like with *Pumping Iron*—we started out cutting that sequentially, and it was impossible to watch. You had bodybuilding competition after bodybuilding competition. And no one wants to watch a sequence of competitions like that, because it's not like football or basketball where you have conflict, and things happen during the main event. With bodybuilding you just have [Bartz flexes his bicep and smiles]. Guys looking good, or trying to look good, some of them not very successfully!

How did you determine how to restructure it?

We went away for four weeks and came back, and suddenly it became clear. Bob Fiore, the codirector, came in and said, "Why do we care about the chronology? I mean: It happened that way, but who cares?" And that's the best thing that can happen in editing: someone reminds you, "Who cares?" You don't have to be a slave to chronology. We *think* we care about chronology, because we were there. But you should only cut to serve the story, to deliver interesting moments that build interest for an audience, scenes that draw them in, that lure them to keep watching, keep them on the edge of their seat. Chronology is useless unless it serves the story.

You threw out the chronological structure and that helped the film?

We figured out how to use the material we hadn't used before in a non-chronological way that worked for the benefit of the overall structure of the film, and not just for a robotic, rote chronology.

You manipulated the order of the events to make a more entertaining story. In documentary films, you enjoy creative license, you're not creating a journalistic report. But where does your need to portray an authentic reality come in?

Editing is all about manipulation—and that's not a bad thing. I mean, you have to pay attention to certain things; you don't want to make it look like something happened that didn't happen. There are ethical boundaries, but outside of that, you have a certain freedom in filmmaking, it's free from the limitations of reality. And you should use that, not shy away from it.

Early filmmakers tried several techniques for telling multiple sides of one story, but parallel editing quickly rose to prominence as the standard method for representing two or more story events occurring at the same time. In 1903's *The Great Train Robbery*, director Edwin Porter, in one of the earliest instances of parallel editing, shows a train robbery from the point of view of the robbers and their victims, cut in parallel so that what might have been two consecutive scenes appear to unfold simultaneously.

Library of Congress control number 00694220.

that frequently helps the story progress. Why are you so attached to that editing approach?

My whole strategy as an editor is to get you on that boat and to go down the river, make it feel like one smooth trip and you're being drawn along. And one thing that can happen is sometimes you'll have two scenes that'll play one after the other—A and B—which, to me, is like getting off the boat, taking a leak on the shore, and then getting back on. It's stopping. It's *stopping*. So, if you can, find a way to intercut those two scenes—and obviously not all scenes can be intercut, there has to be a meaning to the intercutting. But if there is a meaning they can be cut in parallel. Two things happen—one, you're creating one scene rather than two back-to-back scenes. And the other benefit is, you're able to take the best of both scenes—really what you're doing is using scene B as a cutaway for scene A, and scene A as a cutaway for scene B. In other words, you get rid of all the crappy stuff in scene A, because you're now in scene B. When you come back to scene A you can be further along. It's the same reason editors in commercial television love commercial breaks: because the curtain goes down and you can come back up and be somewhere completely different—though I'm very glad I work for HBO and we don't have any commercials!

So, parallel editing allows you to keep up a more energetic and more robust flow to the film by making what appears to be one scene out of two, and by allowing you to cut down the dead spots in the preceding scene by cutting to the next scene and coming back to the preceding scene, scene A, a little bit later on and a little bit deeper into it.

Can you give me an example of how you have used parallel editing in a film?

Well, there's the example of the helicopter arriving and the doctor arriving at the hospital. This was a film, *Operation Lifeline*, that had a scene where a doctor arrived at a hospital, drove up in his—actually, the doctor was a cowboy, and he drove up in his pickup truck. And he went in the hospital, and he went over to his locker, he opened his locker, and he put on his scrubs. And he closed his locker and he went into the operating room. Then cut to a helicopter arriving, a young person being taken off the helicopter, wheeled through the halls into the operating room—scene A, scene B. Now, I just put myself to sleep even *talking* about those two scenes. Those are really boring, but if you cut them together, in parallel, he drives to the hospital, helicopter lands on the roof, he walks into the hospital, door of the helicopter opens and body is taken out, he closes the door of the locker and puts on his scrubs. The gurney's being wheeled through the hall with the young person on it. Doctor walks into the operating room.

At least it has some energy to it. Now it's one scene, and now you've gotten rid of a lot of dead time, and it takes place probably in less time than either one of those scenes took by itself.

It's more dramatic, even as you're describing it, you can see that. The scenes push each other along, visually. Do you use this approach frequently?

It's a very standard technique that's invisible to most people. You're drawing the story and it's a very good way to tell the story, through parallel editing. But obviously there's got to be a relationship between the events—there's either got to be a time relationship, which is the one I just described, or there's got to be an emotional relationship of some kind between the two scenes. Otherwise it won't work.

The Surrogate Audience

What is unique about your editing style? Tell me about a project where you brought something to it that another editor might not have.

I would hope that at the end of a film I've cut you haven't even paid attention to the editing. I don't think I have a signature style, as a lot of editors have. The story, more than anything, is the thing I care about most. That doesn't mean that I make any old sloppy yucky cut, I'm very particular about the kind of cuts I make, because good cutting is indistinguishable from good structure. You can't have good structure and bad editing. Or good cutting and bad structure. I don't consider myself a particularly flashy editor. There are lot of editors I work with whose cutting style I admire a lot more than my own.

Such as?

Paula Heredia. Paula's a brilliant editor. And Juliet Weber. She has a really terrific cutting style. I am devoted to storytelling. I hope that people who see the films I worked say, "Well, I was in that story from the moment it started to the moment it ended."

> *"Good cutting is indistinguishable from good structure."*

Describe the relationship between the editor and the audience.

The editor is the surrogate audience. Good editors and good directors take their ego and they put it in the locker. Lock it away and look at this movie and say, "Is this thing working for a general audience?" It's a very hard thing to do, but you have to.

Geof Bartz and Paula Heredia won the Emmy for best editing for HBO's *In Memoriam: New York City, 9/11/01*.

Photo courtesy of Paula Heredia.

ACADEMY
OF TELEVISION
ARTS &

Geof Bartz winning the editing Emmy in 1980 for *Operation Lifeline*. "I've been up for a number of Emmys, and a bunch of them I've lost to alligators fighting. I think, those alligators!"

Photo courtesy of Geof Bartz.

Geof Bartz in the editing room during *Last Stand Farmer*. "Film crews are made up of different types of people. And editors, I think, are the more introspective types."

Photo by Suzanne Opton, courtesy of Geof Bartz.

When you work on a film for months, or even for years, how do you maintain that editorial distance, and judge how the scenes are serving the audience?

I try to step back from the work I've done at the beginning of the day and watch the film up to that point. And sometimes, at the end of the day, I'll sit back and say, "Is this something I would want to watch?" And if there's something I don't like I'll work on that, because I'm the audience member that actually gets to change this film.

I've got to be honest with you, and I think every editor feels like this, you ask yourself, "Have you done something that you're proud of? Are you proud of that transition? Does it have a little sparkle to it?" All of us are craftspeople. Just like the guy you hire to make the best staircase for your new house, or the guy that's going to make the cabinets for your kitchen. People will look at those cabinets and say, those are really nice cabinets. Those are *great* cabinets. And the reason they're responding to it is because all the little joints are perfectly mortised together. All the little screws are put in exactly in the right alignment. Everything is done meticulously. And you don't notice it. You notice if the cabinet is really lousy, or it's falling down. But you're trying to make a really good cabinet, one that the best carpenters can make. When you come down to it—that's really what we are, in a way, is glorified carpenters. Maybe not even glorified, maybe carpenters are glorified editors.

Paula
Heredia

Editor

Finding Structure, Inventing Form

THE FILMS PAULA HEREDIA HAS WORKED ON REPRESENT A BROAD range of content—from *Finding Christa*, a moving personal story of a woman searching for the daughter she gave up for adoption, which won the 1992 Sundance Jury Award for Best Documentary, to the more recent *In Memoriam: New York City, 9/11/01*, an HBO special for which Heredia shared an Emmy for Best Editing with coeditor Geof Bartz. Independent reviewer Jeff Shannon called *In Memoriam* "one of the most vital documents to emerge after the events of September 11, 2001."

Heredia's projects range from light, entertaining films—such as *Nerve.com: Downloading Sex*, which interweaves footage of a group of sex-obsessed New Yorkers who work for the hip cultural magazine, *Nerve*, with experimental short films and animations about sex—to historical biographies. *The Paris Review: Early Chapters*, for example, traces the editorial career of literary icon George Plimpton, who died in 2003. In 1995, Heredia edited *Unzipped*, directed by

Paula Heredia filmography

Editor Paula Heredia was educated in El Salvador, Costa Rica, Mexico, and England. She now lives in New York, though she often returns to El Salvador, where she teaches and is setting up a graduate-level film program.

Photo courtesy of Paula Heredia.

Douglas Keeve, which brings viewers behind the curtain into the wild world of Isaac Mizrahi, an imaginative fashion designer who resisted commercial impulses and eventually filed for bankruptcy. The film captures the wit and charm of Mizrahi, and reveals the anxiety-filled process as he designs and launches his 1994 fall fashion collection.

The variety in Heredia's portfolio, however, goes beyond its diverse subject matter. The editorial style she's created in many films incorporates techniques, such as original animation, graphics, and effects, that are rarely used in documentaries. Each of the projects she's worked on has a distinct, confident creative vision that exudes an obvious joy for the filmmaking form. Heredia uses a modern approach to editing that goes beyond mere aesthetic impulse; the flair and grace of her cutting style enhances the film while vividly conveying information to the audience.

The conventional wisdom in filmmaking is that effect techniques are not used in documentaries. Traditionally, documentary editors have not altered footage with effects, as they are seen to disturb the straightforward reality captured by the filmmakers. The traditional documentary editor believes her job is to create an experience that transports the audience into a realistic scene, experiencing it as everyday life. Since graphics and effects often bring the viewer out of reality, very few documentary films use them.

But in the late 1980s and '90s, as viewers' sensibilities became more sophisticated, and advances in technology put graphics creation within the budgetary reach of independent filmmakers, editors started to embrace these techniques. Heredia was among the first to pioneer this new approach. In each of the films that Heredia has edited she's brought the subtext of the captured footage to the surface by selectively weaving in composite images, graphics, and animation. In *Nerve.com*, many of the transitional segments are made up entirely of graphics. In *Unzipped*, music, juxtapositions of various film stocks, and title design make the playful, surreal atmosphere of the world of supermodels all the more chic and captivating. The result is both startling and entertaining.

Director

Ralph Gibson: Photographer/Book Artist (2002)

The Paris Review: Early Chapters (2001)

The Couple in the Cage (1997)

Cinematographer

Free Tibet (1998)

Ralph Gibson: Photographer/Book Artist (2002)

The Paris Review: Early Chapters (2001)

Producer

The Couple in the Cage (1997), co-producer

Slings and Arrows (1996), supervising producer

Curious to learn where this style came from, and where this approach to designing a look in postproduction fits into her editorial process, I met Heredia for lunch in a Mexican seafood restaurant in midtown Manhattan. Educated in Costa Rica, Mexico, England, and her native El Salvador, she now lives in New York, though she often returns to El Salvador, where she's teaching and setting up a graduate-level film program.

• • •

How did you first get involved in film?

My formal education was not in filmmaking. I came into filmmaking out of my own search for a medium of expression. My previous education was in fine arts. I came into film thinking of it as something that helps you tell the story, and to tell the story you use whatever you need. That might be a piece of wood, or it might be a piece of metal, or it might be a piece of archival film footage, or a still photograph. It doesn't really matter.

How do you first approach creating a documentary film?

I always think of it as running a farm. You say, "Well, OK, we're going to make a salad." So you go and plant tomatoes, and you go and plant lettuce, and everything that you're going to need. And you spend all this time thinking about: Is it going to be green tomatoes or red tomatoes? Is it going to be this type of lettuce or the other type of lettuce? And you go and plant it, and then you produce all the ingredients, and you come to the kitchen with all these ingredients.

For you, the first part of editing involves collecting or creating the creative elements of the film narrative, before you begin to determine how they will work together.

You still haven't made the salad. You still don't even know what the proportions of that salad are going to be. You don't even know what the final flavor is going to

The program from the exhibition, "Artist and Influence 2001 presents Paula Heredia, Filmmaker."

Courtesy of the Hatch-Billops Collection Inc.

Paula Heredia and Isaac Mizrahi, behind the scenes of *Unzipped*. With *Unzipped*, Heredia says, "I could not approach that documentary in a formal way, because I didn't know where it was going." What she did know was that she needed to preserve the chaotic feel of the film shoot in *Unzipped's* editorial style.

Preparing for the unveiling of Mizrahi's Fall collection in *Unzipped*. Heredia worked on *Unzipped* for months, while the shooting was taking place concurrently. "It was not one of those films that you shoot and then you disappear into a room and digest the material, and then you come up with your conclusions. I had to work with what we knew. We didn't even know what the end was going to be, because the end was going to be determined at the end."

Photo courtesy of Paula Heredia.

be. You only know that you want a salad, and that you have vegetables and ingredients for that salad. And when you start to cut the film, I think of it as starting to cook. You experiment with the ingredients and you find, "Oh, this could be a great tomato salad." Or, "This could be a salad without tomatoes"—regardless of the fact that you have planted all these other vegetables, and planted and collected all these tomatoes. That's, in a nutshell, how I see the editing process.

How do you establish the editing style you'll use on a particular film?

There are a variety of stories that I've been involved with, but each one has had a very different style, because each story dictates that style. It's not that I don't have a style, but the style is not defined by me, or even by the director. The concept might be connected to the director, but the concept and the footage itself is what defines the style.

In the case of *Unzipped*, when I came to see the footage early on, before I had taken the job, the word out there [from other editors who had met with the director] was that there was nothing in that footage, because it was so out of focus, and the camera was all over the place.

What was it like for you during the shooting of *Unzipped*?

For me, the experience during the making of the film was bizarre. Douglas Keeve and Isaac Mizrahi were breaking up. The whole environment was bizarre. Isaac was not part of the editing process, but he was part of the environment. He was around. It was not one of those films that you shoot and then you disappear into a room and digest the material, and then you come up with your conclusions. I had to work with what we knew. We didn't even know what the end was going to be, because the end was going to be determined at the end.

Much of the original footage was not shot by a professional cinematographer, so often you had to give order and style to seemingly chaotic material. I imagine this made the editing process considerably more difficult.

I had all this footage of Paris that had been shot by the director the year before. You know, where you see the footage and you say, "What is that?" It was Super 8 color, it was beautiful, but it was all over the place, zooming in and zooming out, out of focus; the Eiffel Tower and then a motorcycle, and it's just going all around.

After I came in, we brought in Ellen Kuras as a professional cinematographer. Ellen provided the balance in terms of footage that I was getting. Her footage included an interview with Isaac. She shot that interview with him in Paris in the car. He was in black and white, totally beautiful, the window revealed the sky behind him, and Isaac was talking about what he thought of Paris, and how he knew that place. It was very much an expression of who he was.

In *Unzipped*, you intercut a variety of film stocks: Super 8, 16 mm black-and-white, video, and 35 mm color. But it does not come across as haphazard eye-candy; every choice seems to have a narrative purpose. The change in footage helps guide the viewer, as in the end when color is used to show what the fashion show attendees see, while black-and-white is for the behind-the-scenes sequences. How did you use this technique with Isaac, with the Paris footage that was shot earlier?

I figured it's my own fantasy. As an editor, looking at the Super 8 footage, it tells me, "Build something." I could imagine Isaac seeing Paris that way.

The constant movement of the Super 8 footage resembled the point of view of an enthusiastic puppy with a short attention span. You used an artful technique to combine the straight-on interview footage that Kuras had shot with the home-movie-style film. What's the audience end up seeing?

The peacefulness of looking at Isaac through the eyes of Kuras, and then the other layer is Isaac looking out at Paris.

Tension and Style

One of a documentary film editor's challenges is bridging the gap between the often subtle, nuanced story that unfolds as the crew shoots a scene, and what the camera and microphones succeed in capturing. The crew's goal is to shoot footage that will make those nuances obvious and comprehensible to an audience. Sometimes they succeed, sometimes they don't. Nonetheless, it's up to the editor to tell the story as the director sees it, or work with the director in forming a new vision for the narrative. Editors often identify the presence, or lack, of dramatic material in raw footage as "what's there." Heredia describes screening such footage as "reading" the scene. In *Unzipped*, she says, "There was a real contradiction between what the director wanted versus what the footage was saying, and what kind of story could be told from the material."

Creating a documentary is fraught with a variety of tension and conflict that gets resolved (or not) via a complex interplay of personal, creative, and practical negotiations among the various players. To begin with, in most every documentary, there is inherent tension among three versions of the story:

1. The story that the director is trying to capture with the material. This story is usually based on the director's original concept for the film, but it often evolves and changes during shooting as the real life story unfolds in unexpected ways.

2. The story that the editor sees in screening what has been captured by the camera.

3. The edited version of the story, which is the reconciliation between what the editor can structure from the material she's been given, and what the director wants to emphasize: themes, turning points, important exposition of the events or characters, or dramatic moments that will be entertaining and informative to an audience.

In addition to the tension among the different versions of the story, there is tension between truth and drama. While the editor goes about inventing the structure, she must keep the dramatic storyline alive, though she also may feel an ethical responsibility to portray events as they actually happened. In structuring the material, a documentary editor often works like a screenplay writer, charged with crafting the entire narrative and "finding the story" in what is often 100-plus hours of material. With *Unzipped*, Heredia explains, "I could not approach that documentary in a formal way, because I didn't know where it was going." But what she did know, Heredia says, was that she needed to preserve the chaotic feel of the film shoot at the same time she attempted to understand how Mizrahi thought. That was what was driving the style of the footage, and she knew it was essential to capture it in the film's editorial style.

Multiple Perspectives: The Editor's Role

You have a unique view of the editing craft, given that you've worked professionally as an editor, a producer, and a director. How does the collaboration work? Where does the editor fit in?

In the making of the film, there are many actors. There's the director and the producers and the editor, and there's that thing that's going to be filmed. And it's usually either just a concept, or it's footage and a concept. And the director is hoping to find in an editor someone who is going to be able to direct the creative process. Not the film, but the creative process.

The quality I find that is the most useful for an editor is perceptiveness: knowing how to make sense, how to read. I mean *reading* in both senses: reading the psychology of the people who are involved, and reading between the lines of what the footage is saying. And, at the same time, as an editor, you need to be listening to how the footage is being interpreted by everybody around you on the filmmaking team. Nobody's wrong or right. It's just information that you need to absorb while you're viewing the material, and finding the story.

As an editor, you have to guard the story, but you also understand the producer's need to protect the budget. How do you balance these opposing interests?

I think it is very important for an editor to know how to play, because it's all about playing, and being playful. You must develop an environment where the director feels safe about experimenting and trying and failing and finding and going back and trying again with the new information that you have absorbed, over and over—while you go through the editing process. Experimenting is the part of the process that an editor directs, because unfortunately the director is not in the position of being able to be so free, and so apart from the material, from the process, and from the production.

Since directors can rarely be objective with their own material, how do you direct the aesthetic process, as an editor? And how do you balance that with the financial and schedule constraints of independent filmmaking?

Usually, as a director, you get involved in an idea. And to master the process of producing that idea, you need to become thoroughly absorbed in it—either in the concept, or in the production, usually in both. The director's role is in developing what the film is, and what you want to say, and then going out and actually getting the material that is going to help you tell the story. Some directors begin with knowing what story they want to tell; but then they go and shoot and realize they have a choice: either they make the footage fit their original idea, or they allow the concept to be influenced by what the footage is telling them.

> *"There's often more than you think in the footage itself. It's there and the editor has to find it."*

Usually, people start with these vague, general ideas. For example, a filmmaker decides to make a film about a Latino community, and how food influences family relationships. But then she sees she's shot ten hours of a mother cooking and it doesn't seem very interesting. You ask yourself, "What do you have in that scene?" There's often more than you think in the footage itself. You have to believe that if you had that larger concept when you were shooting, it will be expressed through the material you shot, regardless of whether or not you think it's there. It's *there* and the editor has to find it.

On top of that you have the realities of the financing, or the realities of dealing with producers. With independent filmmaking, you have to wear many hats. The process of making every film is thoroughly different. You walk into the editing room where none of the rules from outside apply. The only rule is that you have to do something with the material that's in that room. And you might have an opportunity to go out and pick up a little more clay, but that's as much as it's going to be.

Is that different from a director being charged with capturing the occasional drama—or monotony—of daily life?

As a director, you get to shape the agenda of the film, and of the story. And the editor then tries to work through the problems with your material. It's a discovery when you're editing. Especially with documentaries, it's always a genuine discovery, which requires experimenting.

How has your approach to editing documentaries progressed through the years, as you've gained experience?

Some directors are more or less able to project a picture of the film they want to make. Sometimes I might know that certain ideas are not going to take us where we want to go. And I make an argument for doing it or not doing it. The reaction may be different, depending on the psychology of the moment, or the person that I'm dealing with. Sometimes someone just gets it and I can actually brainstorm and build the story, or we can both build the story verbally. I get into that process and I might be wrong. I learn something else that is going to help me.

Modulations: Cinema for the Ear

Modulations: Cinema for the Ear is a contemporary documentary about the history of electronica and techno music. The subjects range from avant-garde composer John Cage to hip-hop pioneer Afrika Bamabaataa to the ground-breaking German group Kraftwerk, often credited with giving birth to the techno music revolution.

Modulations was another instance of collaborative filmmaking, where the director, Iara Lee, embraced the use of material shot by hundreds of different amateur filmmakers. Your challenge was in making an entertaining, cohesive historical film.

Modulations was an interesting case. Iara Lee's work is about technology and music. She was very interested in two things—one, the fact that this film was shot by many different people in different places, which in terms of concept was a great idea, but in terms of the footage was horrible, because the quality of the footage was *really* bad. And the quality of the interviews was not very good, either. There was not this consistency of one director being on location, having a view of what they want to get out of the character.

Since so many of the people were well known in that world of techno music, she wanted to have them all represented. That meant, there were hundreds of interviews for me to screen. Most of the people were great musicians, I'm sure, but they were not great people to talk about their own craft, or art, or history. So it was a very difficult project and, on top of that, it was a very complex story.

As an editor, reading the footage helps. For me, seeing all that film, it felt like a roller coaster. It just went up and down, and you had an experience. You had a sense of all these things that went on; you had an amazing experience, but this was not a lesson in history.

By experimenting with the material Lee gave you, you found a solution to telling the story.

I tried to fill certain holes by using graphics when I had no other choice. We had to have something that at least tells you about all these movements, because it was not coming out in a way that's understandable. Lee went back and shot anything I wanted, because the original material was just interviews. So you sit down and say, "OK, I'm going to make this happen." And then you say, "Well, but I need a tomato since this is going to be tomato soup. At least I need the tomato." And then someone goes and gets a tomato.

You don't restrict creative brainstorming because of financial constraints.

Let's not stop ideas because they might require production, or money. It's important to ask, freely, "If we have a problem, what if we were to solve it by doing *x*?" And then you play with that idea, and you build it, and you come to the conclusion that, no, it's not going to make a difference in what you're trying to do, then that's the end of it. But if it's the right idea, then you deal with the production aspect at that point, and figure out if it's both feasible and worth the expense.

Free Tibet

Free Tibet is a political film that Heredia codirected and edited with recording artist Adam Yauch of the Beastie Boys. The project was spearheaded by Yauch, with the goal of leveraging the Beastie Boys' fame and their concert performance to draw attention to the human rights tragedies in Tibet.

Was it possible to employ your philosophy of directing with Yauch, who was both a celebrity and the financial backer of the film?

Free Tibet was another film where the editing style was developed to serve the film. It was a difficult project because it was a political documentary. I mean, it was actually the first time that I was making a propaganda movie with money.

It seems like *Free Tibet* would be a challenge to edit because of the discrepancy between the material you had to work with, and the political and social circumstances the director wished to portray. The footage was centered on a Beastie Boys concert that the band put on as a fund-raiser.

There were all these kids that came really for the music, not for the Tibetans. So that was one of the ingredients. The other ingredient was very devastating repression footage in Tibet, and the third ingredient was these beautiful shots of Tibet. How do you cook all of that together to make a powerful movie and a powerful statement?

What was your relationship with Adam Yauch like?

Adam was—from the editor's point of view—the dream director. He actually fired the first director and then took over. I think that it's one of those things that happen; Adam was the only one who actually could do that film. He was the one who had the heart to do it, and the vision. And his vision obviously had not been translated to the first director that he fired. So it was very difficult at the time, but then, when he took over, it was incredible. Every day we had brainstorming, and you

[continued on page 286]

Editing Portraits

A documentary editor shapes the film narrative. With a biographical film that means being accountable for telling someone's life story. Getting the story right is an enormous responsibility; making the film entertaining and watchable, which is the larger job of the editor, requires careful balance.

Heredia has worked on several nontraditional biographical documentaries, where the film's story consisted of a central character's dramatic experiences. The Sundance-heralded film *Finding Christa* documents filmmaker Camille Billops' heartbreaking search for the daughter she gave up for adoption. In *The Vagina Monologues*, performer Eve Ensler balances comedy with serious feminist issues through the use of stories about female genitalia. *The Paris Review: Early Chapters* uses the backdrop of the founding of the famous literary magazine, *The Paris Review*, to tell the story of its unflappable founder, George Plimpton.

"This whole genre of films that I have either edited or directed myself," Heredia tells me, "I call 'portraits.' They have been my most formal documentaries, even though they have their own style. I think that part of the reason I'm good at making por-trait films is that they are all about people who are alive. So it's not an archival film, where you don't have to talk to the people left behind. There's nobody telling you, 'I don't want him to be portrayed that way.'"

Documentary editors pore over material for weeks and months, digesting the meaning of what they are given: film clips, photographs, interviews, transcripts. In making a biographical film, through viewing the subject's life artifacts, the editor comes to know the person intimately, but great editing always requires distance. The interpersonal dynamics of making a biographical or autobiographical docu-mentary with the living subject of the film can be challenging. Because the editor's job is to represent the interests of the audience, she is focused entirely on the quality of the storytelling; the director, on the other hand, is inevitably invested in how he or she will come off. With every cut, the editor makes conjectures and statements about the person's character; as an empathetic person, an editor cannot help but be distracted by the nagging question, "What will the subject think of this portrayal?"

Mayor Rudolph Giuliani, Paula Heredia, and Sheila Nevins, president of HBO Documentary and HBO Family, attend the premiere of *In Memoriam: New York City, 9/11/01*, at Lincoln Center. "I came into the project with a universal feeling for what the emotions of that event meant," says Heredia. "In a way, I was making a film that was expressing many, many, other stories of suffering that were reflected in that event. In that sense, for me, it was also a healing. Because making films is a therapeutic process."

Photo courtesy of Paula Heredia.

Kevin Segalla
View from Chambers Street

Mi-Kyung Heller
View from Franklin Street

Pilots Walsh and Hayes
NYPD Helicopter Video

Geof Bartz, your coeditor, joined the project toward its end.

We were quite behind, and he did something that was pretty amazing to me. We had interviewed many people—we interviewed everybody on Giuliani's staff. We didn't use much of that footage, but we interviewed everybody, because we donated all the interviews and all the archives to the museum. One of the people that Sheila interviewed was Giuliani's secretary, who lost her husband, a firefighter, on 9/11. What was amazing about that interview was that she had never talked to anybody, and she was in that state in which she was holding back everything.

Then, as the interview proceeded, the widow's emotions came out for the first time.

Yes, anger and everything. What happened with that interview was that one of the tapes had incredible sound problems. But in watching it you could tell it was an amazing interview. We were able to use the transcript tapes and get something that was pretty bad, but was there.

After screening the material you cut using the interview with poor audio quality, HBO recognized the sound problem. Nevins decided she needed to interview the woman again, to capture better sound quality.

How long after the first interview did the second interview take place?

It was about two weeks later. But when Sheila interviewed her again, she was a totally different person: physically and emotionally.

In the first interview the emotional dam broke, and her feelings were captured on film, but by the second interview…

She had *spoken*. She was still suffering, but she had spoken. She told the same story.

From *In Memoriam: New York City, 9/11/01.* This film was a collaboration between HBO and the Mayor's Office of New York. "We were using material from many people who simply shot footage out of their windows, and footage that the networks and news organizations had shot and collected, but never used. Everyone had these images of two towers: hours and hours of that shot. But when you see things in real time, the bad thing is that you're reliving that, but the good thing is that you feel you were part of it, that you can understand what happened. It's not just a fragment of an emotion. You can go through the whole emotion in real time, and live it."

Photos courtesy of Kevin Segalla, Mi-Kyung Heller, and the NYPD.

It seems your fundamental conception of a documentary is quite different from other filmmakers. Do you think your background in fine arts provides you with a unique perspective?

There are many different concepts of what a documentary is. I think that the only way to be honest, the only reason a documentary is honest, is because the filmmaker felt that what he's saying is honest. That doesn't mean it's right, it's wrong, it's history, it's reality, or it's not. There are things that one can question about a documentary: maybe you should have done this, or should have done that. But in the end, the only person who can calculate what should be in the film is the filmmaker.

Paula Heredia and Geof Bartz share the 2002 Creative Emmy Award for Best Editing for *In Memoriam: New York City, 9/11/01*. "The whole film is about recreating the events by recreating the emotions of that day. As an editor, every time I see the film, I see every scene, every cut, thousands of times. The only way I know if it works or if it doesn't work is if, in watching it, I live that moment, live that frame, live that cut."

Photo courtesy of Paula Heredia.

Larry
Silk

Editor

Using the Mystery of What Comes Next

FOR THOSE FAMILIAR WITH DOCUMENTARY FILM AND TELEVISION HISTORY, Lawrence Silk, A.C.E., known to friends and colleagues as Larry, is a legend. In recent years, when he took an editing job at *National Geographic*, producer Pam Hogan wrote a memorandum to the entire company that began, "You may know by now that we have a renowned documentary filmmaker temporarily in our midst: acclaimed film editor Larry Silk…" So that her production team would appreciate the historical significance of Silk's work, Hogan set up a screening of several films he'd edited, and invited him to discuss them with her and the team.

In 1953—although, as Silk says, "there were hardly any documentaries being made at that time"—he took a job in New York with Richard Leacock, "the brilliant soon-to-be cinema verité shooter," and Willard Van Dyke. Van Dyke's films from the 1930s had been an inspiration to Silk as a young boy, and stimulated his interest in editing. Silk worked as an assistant editor with

Leacock on his pioneering documentary work for *Omnibus*, the first network television magazine, where he "learned from those guys to respect work, and the pleasure of accomplishing creative work." And so began a career that would span 50 years as an editor, as an NYU film-editing instructor, and—over the decades—as mentor to dozens of the documentary world's burgeoning upstarts: assistants, interns, producers, and editors.

The first television project on which Silk received an editor credit was NBC's landmark program, *Sit In*. "It was 1960, the heyday of television trying to serve public interest," he recalls. *Sit In* broke new ground in two ways: with content—"It was the first time any network had ever dealt with the discrimination of blacks, where you saw black people sticking up for themselves"—and with a very dramatic editing style. Producer Robert Young's interviews made possible "creating a drama, where the story was done by editing."

These nascent attributes eventually became the hallmark of Silk's editing practice, unifying his diverse filmography. Nearly every film he's cut is one of substance, grace, and integrity. Moreover, each addresses a contemporary issue facing society, crafted in a substantive way: usually experiential, personal, and classically dramatic. "I think audience. I think, what do people *need* to really get hooked into this story? Whenever I can, I like to keep it a bit mysterious—and *use* the mystery of what will happen next."

Over the past several decades, Silk has collected numerous awards for his editing work, for programs

"When you're making feature documentaries, as opposed to dramatic feature films, you don't have rape, you don't have murder, you don't have real mystery, you hardly have any humor. Certainly you don't have comedy—unless, it's about comedians or something. You don't have any of these great elements that feature editors have. So you've got to work within the material that really excites you. And that's the secret of editing documentaries. You've got to find some way into it —unless it's a film that's totally academic."

Photo courtesy of Larry Silk.

on all the broadcast networks as well as PBS and HBO. For television, he edited
and consulted on several Emmy Award-winning series, such as *Lifeline, Childhood,
Healing and the Mind with Bill Moyers*, and the Moyers PBS series *Addiction*.

However, the work Silk finds most personally rewarding is the creative trial of editing unscripted feature-length documentaries. He has collaborated on several films
with Academy Award-winning director Barbara Kopple, including *Fallen Champ:
The Untold Story of Mike Tyson* (which took home a Primetime Emmy Award), *The
Hamptons,* and *Wild Man Blues,* which follows Woody Allen and his jazz band on
a tour of Europe. Each of these documentary features is full of surprising moments,
many with narrative twists and turns. Silk's editing skillfully and subtly entertains
the audience by bringing to life multidimensional characters that deepen the subtext and elevate personal struggles. Most important, the dramatic casting of these
characters in the edit draws in the audience in compelling fashion.

For example, Kopple's Oscar-winning *American Dream* explores the complex
position of the unions in the contemporary workforce—from the inside. In
addition to its Academy Award, *American Dream* was a triple prizewinner at
the Sundance Film Festival, and winner of the Directors Guild of America,
International Documentary Association, and National Society of Film Critics "Best
Documentary" awards.

Among Silk's other documentary feature credits are the groundbreaking film
Pumping Iron, featuring a young Arnold Schwarzenegger; *Johnny Cash: The Man,
His World, His Music;* and *Marjoe*. But beyond the accolades, it's Silk's innate sense
of character and his nose for compelling story lines that keep him prolific. "In
screening dailies, I look for footage that's both visually beautiful—beautifully,
sensitively shot—and *reveals* something: interesting experiential stuff. I look for
material I can edit, that I can make something out of, so that audiences feel that
moment, the *life* of that moment."

● ● ●

The Origins of Documentary

What initially drew you to documentary editing?

I was inspired by documentaries when I was very young—the early documentary filmmakers Pare Lorentz and Willard Van Dyke, and films of the 1930s that were made by the government of FDR, the Farm Security Administration, the Dorothea Lange photographs—all of that.

Before I knew anything about what editing was, I was inspired by films like *The River* and *The City*. I didn't know anything about editing, but the rhythms of the editing were very dynamic. In fact, they were copied by Hollywood moviemakers. They copied films like *The City* shot for shot and cut for cut, capturing the rhythm of New York City, brilliant sequences. But I didn't know *that* was "editing." I just knew I was very attracted and inspired by those films.

What was inspiring about them?

Not only was the editing very impressive, even though I didn't know it *was* editing. But the music was by Aaron Copland and Virgil Thompson. The narration was read by a fine Shakespearean actor, Morris Karnovsky, who was very famous then—beautifully written. It was very poetic narration. In later years, I had a chance to use clips from *The City* in another film I edited; a long time later, in the '60s we were making this film called *The Rise of the New Town Movement*, showing how the megalopolis had swallowed up the surrounding area around these places, but they still existed. And I showed some of the Mumford ideas that were in *The City* [1939; directed by Ralph Steiner and Willard Van Dyke and written by Lewis Mumford from a story by Pare Lorentz].

How did *The City* influence the way you edited *The Rise of the New Town Movement* 30 years later?

Actually, I made matched edits from *The City*. I matched scenes of a kid biking through an underpass in one of these lovely new towns, in Radburn, New Jersey,

in 1938, and I cut that shot to an underpass in 1965. We had a lot of fun. I also
gave narration credit to those important people that had worked on the original by
Pare Lorenz, to show how important it was then.

When did you get your start in documentaries?

In 1953, I ended up getting a job with Willard Van Dyke himself. He had a studio.
And Ricky Leacock, the brilliant soon-to-be cinema verité shooter, was working
there. He was the cameraman for Robert Flaherty on many of his projects. He's a
historian. So I worked with these very interesting documentary film guys, and I got
a sense of their commitment to the craft, and their commitment to social issues. I
was somewhat left wing myself at that time. It was a time when, especially in film
work, *nobody* talked about their political views. It was a very repressive time.

How did you know they were supportive of left wing ideals, then?

Well, we talked obliquely about what they knew about life. The only time we
started talking about politics was when the Army-McCarthy hearings took place,
and [Army attorney] Joseph Welch took [anti-Communist crusader Sen. Joseph]
McCarthy apart at the televised hearings. And suddenly McCarthy was a laugh-
ingstock. It broke the dam. Suddenly, you could talk about it. Especially when CBS

started challenging McCarthy with Ed Murrow. When Murrow did a show on McCarthy, *that* broke the dam. Everybody found the courage to talk.

But Ricky did a film about the tent theater shows that were dying in Iowa and Missouri and Arkansas, which had traditionally traveled through the rural areas like carnivals. The tent shows did continuing stories about a Boston Brahman-type bride to a country bumpkin, in which they made fun of the Boston aristocracy. It was something the farmers loved. They just ate it up. They were like soap operas, only they were comic—making fun of the Eastern establishment.

Leacock filmed a dying folk tradition. Were these pieces aired on television?

Yes. This was before PBS. CBS had an early show called *Omnibus*, and Alistair Cooke was the host. It was a Sunday show, like *60 Minutes*. It was a magazine show—the first magazine show. And they had documentary segments—that's what it was built on. Leacock shot it and edited it, and I was his assistant editor.

You enjoyed working with Leacock? He was a mentor, of sorts, to you?

Yes, I loved working with him. It was so pure, his interest, he was so excited about it. He taught me darkroom techniques. I learned how to use Tri-X film, the high-speed black and white film in those days, which had just come out. I rolled it off into cassettes. I bought a 35mm camera, and started taking photographs and learned about the darkroom because I was inspired by Ricky. I learned a lot from him.

What did you learn from him?

I was in my 20s, working with those guys in '54 to '56 or '57, and Kevin Smith was there, he was production manager, assistant cameraman, whatever, and he later became the producer of the physics films on which I became an editor for the first time. I learned from those guys to respect the work, and the pleasure of accomplishing creative work.

Sit In: The Dawn of Public Interest Television

Eventually, you came to New York.

I started working in television documentaries when I came to New York, worked on the NBC *White Paper* in 1960, which was the heyday of television trying to serve public interest, first and foremost.

Why was television focused on serving the public interest?

Because of the quiz show scandal [which revealed that game shows were fixed]. Television was so humiliated by the press attacks. The press doesn't have that kind of power anymore over television, but at that time they did. And the press went after them, and the public went after them, and Congress went after them.

People learned that the game show producers were feeding certain contestants the answers, so they would predetermine the winners. And when this came out in the late 1950s, the networks lost their credibility with the American public.

They funded documentary programs to redeem their reputation?

Yes. [Federal Communications Commission Chairman] Newt Minnow called it, "The vast wasteland of network television." So they immediately pulled their socks up and started doing public affairs in 1960, and suddenly the American people discovered poverty. They did a show on migrant workers in Florida, *Harvest of Shame*, which had enormous power. And I joined *White Paper*, which was NBC's answer to CBS. And I edited *Sit In*. Some clips were utilized in the PBS series *Eyes on the Prize* from my edit of 20 years earlier.

Why was *Sit In* such an important television program?

Sit In was a landmark film because it was the first time any network had ever dealt with the discrimination of blacks. Actually, they were called "Negroes" at the time.

The 1960 NBC documentary *Sit In* broke new ground in two ways: In content—"It was the first time any network had ever dealt with the discrimination of blacks," Silk says, "where you saw black people sticking up for themselves"—and in style, "telling a drama, where the story was done by editing."

But it was the first time on a nationwide network you saw black people sticking up for themselves. Robert Young was the producer. So Bob Young was hired by NBC *White Paper*, and Albert Wasserman, who came from CBS, introduced *Sit In*. He was the executive producer and Young was the director/producer, and it was so controversial. It showed passive resistance. It all happened at the lunch counters. And they eventually achieved a great victory.

What was the style of programming, what was the editorial style?

The editorial style was rather unique. Bob Young was a young and adventurous filmmaker, a very ambitious young guy. And *very* persistent! And I had an opportunity to cut in a unique way because of the way he operated—he went to the Southern NBC affiliates and he said, "I want to see what you've got on the sit in strikes that just took place six months ago. I want to see all your footage." But they didn't show him everything.

Why not?

Because they were afraid of being sued. The payoff of which is that it was blacked out in the South. Meaning, they didn't show it. Largely blacked out, not entirely.

Why were they afraid of it?

For the first time, nationwide television was revealing discrimination against Negroes. And, Negroes fighting for their rights as American citizens. That was the

"I

Why

I thir
inter
that s
head

You
head
cam
time

Yes.
cutt
goin
ing
wer
righ
up.
ma
"Bo
got
lev

To
m:

Pr
vo

W
a

first time it was *ever* shown on television. No network ever had done that. So they were afraid of advertisers, they were afraid of public reaction. People saying, "I don't want to watch this goddamn fucking Communist shit." Pardon me.

Sit In was a big risk for NBC. Who were they afraid of most?

They were afraid of the reaction of the white community. And, they were afraid of segregationist sentiment. After all, it was a long custom in the South. It came from God, practically. To see young Negroes from divinity school or Fisk University students, white divinity students and Fisk University students in the black school, in Nashville, demonstrating, breaking the segregation laws! Sitting at lunch counters in Woolworth's, for God's sake! It was shocking.

Was it dangerous, poking around, to try to uncover the story?

Robert Young was very gutsy. He got a hold of the footage he found of the demonstrations and of the hoodlums attacking these people at the lunch counter. How did he find it? He walked around in the local NBC affiliate station and opened cabinets. He had this baby face, very innocent. "What's this old film? Oh, what's this, let's look at it." And he saw what it was. He could just tell by looking at it—he got ahold of all the stuff that they were afraid to give him of their news coverage of those events.

That's investigative journalism. And he did it so innocent-like.

Why?

Because every cut is a disturbance of reality. So the trick is to cut artfully, so the cut gives you more than the disturbance it creates. That is a basic element in my whole theory of editing.

"I want you to write a paragraph that I can nail to the wall."

Can you describe that theory in more detail?

When you cut, you go to something even more exciting. It could even be the same kind of moment, and then people won't even know it's a cut. They won't even *see* it. Because just as they're beginning to smell boredom, you're leaping into the essence of what's happening. You're giving them more and more essence of what you know. But at the same time you're trying to maintain the real time theory.

You want the audience to feel as though they are watching events as they actually happened, but you avoid boring them by focusing their attention—through selection—on the dramatic focal point of the scene.

I'm trying to give the audience the experience of what's happening in a way that you would *want* to perceive it—approximating the experience of being there, but using the dramatic excitement. That's why they're buying the film in the first place.

Why *are* they watching?

Because they know there's something there. It's not just voyeurism. They want to really *be* in another world, another experience, another situation that they can only have this way: through film.

It's the editor's job to transport an audience into that other world.

The editor's relationship to the audience is—you've heard me say it—we're the proxy for audiences. Editors, at least me, and I'm sure any other good editor, want to know when we begin editing: what's this film, why are you making it? What do you want to do with it? What do you think it's going to do? I'm very concerned with that. What's the *point* of it?

Can you give me an example?

When I was working on a project years ago with Jack Willis, I said, "I want you to write a paragraph that I can nail to the wall. One paragraph about what you want this film to do. And if I don't agree with it, of course I'll argue with you, but if I do agree with you I'll do what I can to look for that in the material," the material that I think will be germane to your story line.

Marjoe: The Appeal of a Rascal

You've told me you enjoy working on feature-length documentaries more than you do television programs, because you can delve deeper into the story, and build real characters.

Marjoe was a character who really interested you.

With *Marjoe*, I knew we wanted to use his character for a dramatic effect. And the effect of the character Marjoe Gortner, the Pentecostal evangelist, was the fact that he had the charm of a rascal. And, as I asked the audiences at Cannes and my editing students at NYU—it had just won an Oscar when I got hired as a teacher there, they were all excited about seeing it—"How many people liked him?" Half the class liked him. "How many people don't like him?" Half the class didn't like him. So I said, "Well, you know, I had mixed feelings about him." I realized this is a rascal, and like all rascals, he's very charming, and the world would be much worse off without them.

In *Snapping: America's Epidemic of Sudden Personality Change* authors Flo Conway and Jim Siegelman wrote about Sarah Kernochan's film, *Marjoe*, saying, "Marjoe Gortner was the first evangelical preacher to blow the whistle on his profession." The film was controversial, in that it revealed many tricks of the trade. "Marjoe is one of those frank films that delves deeply into sensitive areas of American morality that slip over the line into profiteering."

Photos courtesy of Sarah Kernochan.

As an editor, you need to relate to the characters.

And he was entertaining these people as he was taking their money. They were getting their money's worth out of him. So, that's one way of relating to character. I wouldn't want to have dinner with him, charming as he was. I didn't trust him at all.

What was your relationship with Marjoe Gortner during the production of the film? Did you know him, personally?

The people who were producing the film, and were partnered with him, would not allow him into the editing room.

Why?

Because they knew that he would try and charm me to the point where he could control the editing.

Was he afraid they were doing an exposé? Why did he want to control the editing process?

Because he didn't trust anybody! That was Marjoe's position in life: He didn't trust anybody. And he was shocked when he liked the film, and he was laughing all the way through it, even the places where he was dunning people.

Pumping Iron: Creating Substantive Story Lines and Archetypal Characters

When you start on any new project, the director has a certain perspective on the story that comes from his or her experience shooting in the field and forming personal relationships with the subjects. But you have only what the camera captured, what an audience could potentially see. So, as an editor, how do you manage to reconcile the story the director wishes to tell with the film story line the footage provides for you to cut?

You portray the characters in that film as nuanced figures, with many facets. What did George Butler see in Schwarzenegger?

He loved his rascally personality, the charm of it—and we did, too—his competitive zeal. But he was also hardworking. You see that in the film, too, how hard he worked. It wasn't just noise from him. Butler thought he was a very admirable character. He probably liked him visually, thought he was beautiful.

Tell me about your collaboration with Butler.

He didn't have a lot to say about the way we put it together, that I can remember. But he did come up with the idea of the opening scene, which we all give him tremendous credit for. The little ballet dance teacher, teaching Schwarzenegger and Franco Columbo how to pose, at the very beginning of the film? Terrific idea. And it was well done.

Why was it a terrific idea?

Well, it was an invitation. It was, like, "Oh, look at these giants. Look at the contrast." And the little ballet dance teacher was showing Arnold how to pose, and they were very earnest about it. It was funny. To start with a funny scene about a subject which—at that time, especially—a lot of people were put off by, it was a great idea.

At the time it was made, the subject was taboo?

Even I reacted that way, initially. When I got a copy of the book, *Pumping Iron*, and they first tried to talk me into working on the film, I had it in a brown paper bag in the subway. I'm embarrassed to admit it, but on the cover it's a guy practically naked, posing. And most people would know that was a gay interest.

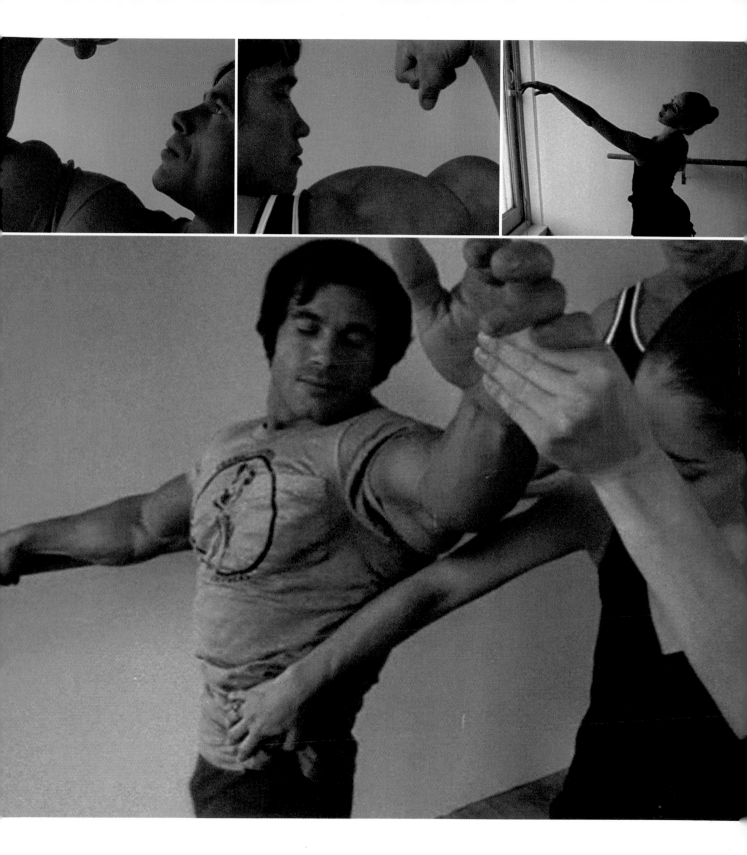

You didn't want people to see you reading it, for fear of what they might infer about your sexuality?

Gay interest. Sitting there reading something only gays are interested in. My homophobia, it brought it out. That was a different time. We had different feelings about bodybuilding at that time. So we were all aware of that.

Was it a problem that you were unfamiliar with the subject, aside from Butler's book?

I think producers who are smart seem to understand it's best to hire an editor who's not in love with the character or the subject, he might have even a negative view of it, but a certain amount of curiosity. Rather have an editor like that than have an editor who's an aficionado of the subject.

Did that affect the way you approached the editing, your prejudice regarding the subject matter, and what people inferred about the subject?

One of the greatest things that happened in the production of that film was in Peter Davis's interview of Arnold. Peter Davis is to all appearances a very preppy, intellectual Harvard guy; very proper. But he says, "Arnold, you know that you have a tremendous amount of interest among people who are homosexuals." (They didn't use the word *gay* in those days.) "What's your feeling about that? When you're getting ready to compete, and all these gay guys are standing there admiring you and taking pictures. How do you feel about that?"

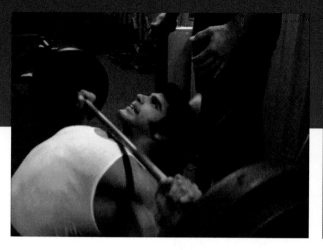

Arnold surprised us all with his answer. He said, "I think it's great! Let them enjoy themselves!" You have to love him for that. It's a very European reaction, I thought. Americans would have that prissy feeling. But for him, it was simple. It was such a gutsy reaction, but absolutely natural to him. Anyway, I just love that.

I don't remember that moment.

Well, unfortunately, it's not in the film. They had beautiful stuff that's not in these films. There was no big issue about confronting homophobia, at that time, so we left it out. Editors call that "killing your babies."

What else do you miss, that was left on the cutting room floor?

We had a wonderful sequence with Arnold in South Africa talking to his mentor, Reg Park. He's a South African who is very wealthy. He had turned bodybuilding into a very successful career for himself, owning gyms and so on. In the scene, he has this beautiful house with a swimming pool. And there are these two guys who are half naked, with bathing suits, like a couple of porpoises playing in the swimming pool. It was a great scene. Then he sits down, and it's the only time you see Arnold really listening to his mentor, as his mentor gives him all his theories of success. It's a wonderful scene and revealing another dimension of Arnold.

Why did you cut it?

It was killing the flow. We didn't want to see him with Reg Park, we wanted to build up toward the competition. And they weren't talking about the competition, they were talking about that world that they were in, and their ambitions, and the greed. It's great. If you were doing a documentary that was a more political one, it might have been useful, but that's not what we were doing.

What was *Pumping Iron* really about? What was its subtext to you?

I saw the film as a film about fathers and sons, actually. We took these characters, and we really made them prototypes of what they were. Arnold, the super smart, competitive rascal, who really worked hard—to back up his rascality—and was admirable in many ways. Certainly in smarts he was admirable. And Louis Ferrigno was interesting, too. His story was the strongest epitome of the theme of fathers and sons, because of his dad and him, their whole relationship was foreground. With Arnold, it was more background. And then Franco Columbo I saw as—and we all felt this—the love interest in the film.

You hit a creative roadblock, during the editing.

We just got so tired of working on it. It was like a moving mass of very nice sequences. So I declared a hiatus. I said, "Let's take at least a month off and then come back and see where we're at with it." And we came back, and we figured it out immediately. Sometimes you need to do this when working on something that's complex, and seems daunting.

American Dream: Complex, Righteous Characters

You've collaborated on several films with Barbara Kopple: *Fallen Champ: The Untold Story of Mike Tyson*; *The Hamptons*; and *Wild Man Blues*. The Academy Award-winning *American Dream* shows the complex position of the unions in the contemporary workforce from the inside.

Yes, it show the excessively righteous and loser position of the unions.

Did you know what the film would be about when you started?

No, we didn't know. Barbara shot the whole meat-packing industry. She was working for years out there, in the wilds of Minnesota and Kansas and Iowa, gathering very human stories. We didn't know when we started editing it what we were supposed to do. She didn't want to tell us—maybe because she didn't know.

She works in a more classic direct cinema style, organically discovering the intent of the story?

Perhaps that's why she likes to hire me as an editor. Because I think about the purpose, the meaning behind it.

American Dream **is a sharp political story. However, the material is not presented as political issues, but shown through characters' lives. When you and I first met, on an editing job, I was struck by how perceptive you were in referring to the characters. Most of them you had never met in person, but you talked about them with great familiarity—their personality traits, their backgrounds, sense of humor, character flaws, and motivations—as if they were your close friends. You have an innate understanding of what makes people tick, of what's behind their seemingly pedestrian actions.**

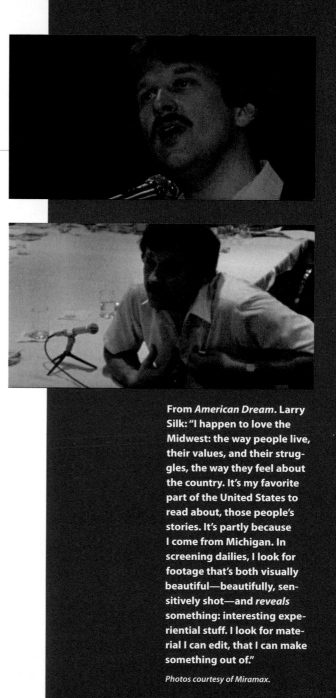

From *American Dream*. Larry Silk: "I happen to love the Midwest: the way people live, their values, and their struggles, the way they feel about the country. It's my favorite part of the United States to read about, those people's stories. It's partly because I come from Michigan. In screening dailies, I look for footage that's both visually beautiful—beautifully, sensitively shot—and *reveals* something: interesting experiential stuff. I look for material I can edit, that I can make something out of."

Photos courtesy of Miramax.

Describe the connection you felt to the characters in *American Dream*.

I happen to love the Midwest: the way people live, their values and their struggles, the way they feel about the country. It's my favorite part of the United States to read about, those people's stories. It's partly because I come from Michigan.

So *American Dream* was interesting for me, as a side look at the values in the Midwest, and in that battle that was going on between the local union and their leaders in Minnesota, fighting for their status with the mother ship of the company. The story focused on the first plant that Hormel built to begin their expansion, where the people had felt privileged to work, but they were treated in a patronizing way. The population was almost entirely Minnesotans, of mostly Nordic background—very righteous culture. I think all parts of the country have that righteous vein, but that particular ethnicity has got more righteousness than many—maybe to its detriment, I sense. You could see any of those stories of Mark Twain, full of that sense of righteousness, and belief that fairness was all that mattered.

Their opponent was the director of the meatpacking division of the international union, Louis Anderson, who was up from the slaughterhouse pits of Iowa and Chicago and places like that. To me, he represented the other aspect of the Midwest: hard-bitten realism; cynical, skeptical talk. He talks about when you go on strike, it's a war with the company. And unless you can take money out of their pockets you'll be standing there with your dicks hanging out, and watching the scabs go by. He said that in the film.

I recall. That's quite a visual!

Ha!

You used your understanding of who these two men were—two different representations of Midwestern personalities—to contrast the competing camps: One was interested in leveraging the fundamental lack of fairness in the meat packers's pay cuts, the other was trying to persuade the rank-and-file to meet the company in traditional union-management negotiations, rather than threaten them with the strike. How did determining those personality dynamics allow you to develop dramatic conflict in the film?

There was this contrast. The striking local's elected leader, Jim Guyette, said of the fairness issue, "We can blast the media with it! Hormel, which prides itself on its public relations, they're going to cave, man. They won't be able to take the publicity." But he was just totally wrong. Anybody who understood how the system works would know that money is more important than anything else.

Louis never talked about fairness. I mean, he talked about it as just political rhetoric, but he was talking about reality and strength. And so that, to me, was very Midwest also. Big city Midwest: Chicago! Omaha!

The meatpackers in *American Dream* had a strong personal connection to their work, which translated to a loyalty to Hormel.

These people had expected to be the *darlings* of this Hormel plant. They expected that they would always be treated that way. That's sort of a side look about character. I could be totally wrong about it, but that's the way I saw it. It's my theory about the Midwest, that those are interesting elements in a Midwestern American story.

Tell me about how you put the film together in the cutting room. Were you making requests for coverage, to create a nuanced story line?

[Coeditor] Tom Haneke and I did lots of research, and we also ended up doing the vital voice-over interviews. Barbara didn't have time for them, and she didn't know what we really needed. She said, "You guys know what questions you need people to answer. So why don't *you* interview the principals?" And we did.

Career Advice for Budding Editors

When you discuss the history of the craft of editing, it's impossible to divorce that conversation from the long tradition of close apprentice/mentor relationships. Most great editors working in film and television today learned their craft through personal oral history, the guidance and example of senior editors. Much of that guidance centers around storytelling strategies, cutting style, and editorial structure. But part of what is passed on is simply practical, life lessons on how to manage your working life in what can be a challenging corner of the entertainment industry. Many of the things Larry Silk has taught me and many other editors and producers over the years have influenced our daily work habits. Here, and later, in *Approaching the Edit*, I've shortened down to generalized principals some of the advice he's lent, expanded by Silk's own words.

Advocate for the audience first, but remain open to new ideas.

"With the accessibility of computer-based editing, the editing profession is now very different. Very few editors are in a situation that I find myself in occasionally, thank God, where I have a lot more control over what I'm doing. In becoming an editor today, you're going to become an editor in a place where editors have very little to say. Because most of the work is not editor-intensive, or it's not known to be, and maybe the producer and directors have as much intensity in the editing as the editors do now, because there are young people who know how to operate the equipment. And the producer sits there and says, 'It's should be this way, that's no good, it should *that* way.' You know, *they're* the editors.

"But, on the film I just edited about the paraplegic fighting for stem cell research, this first-time director—who is also the film's subject—suggested this wonderful thing at the very end of the end credits. In red type, 'This film could not have been made without President George W. Bush.' *Perfect*. I liked that. He had some other suggestions that helped me in restructuring. So he really contributed. And the thing is, if people have an idea, you owe it to *yourself*—not to them—to consider it. Even though you have all the arguments in the world against it, it's like kicking a radio when it's got a little static and it suddenly comes clear. Their solution may not be the right one. But it might be pointing to something that is deep in your own brain, and it can stimulate another. So you should always give consideration to what anybody says, I don't care what it is."

Work with producers and directors you respect, and who respect you.

"Ideally, somebody who knows how to get the best out of the people they're working with. And who has an idea of the real potential of the subject. And maybe has a real intensity in terms of how they approach it. It's not like a term paper. It's like an opus. It's like they're hanging their ego on it. It's really important."

Screen documentaries, be curious and excited to learn.

"See as many films as you can, and develop a love of what documentaries are. Showing *real* reality that can be interpreted in some way that tells some truth."

Don't be afraid to step away, and gain perspective.

"During *Pumping Iron*, we were struggling with the structure. It was like a moving mass of very nice sequences so we took a hiatus. I said, 'Let's take at least a month off and then come back and see where we're at with it.' And we came back, and we figured it out immediately. You have to pull yourself away sometimes. You have to begin to see what's getting in your way."

Why were you attached to that scene? And why did you end up cutting it?

It was totally charming. It's 2 minutes of absolute embarrassment, tension, charm, everything. It was probably the last thing I took out. I was ordered to get it down from 94 to 90 minutes, and I couldn't see anything else to take out. Both Barbara and I mourn the loss of that scene. "We always kill our babies," as the editors say in this business. The things we love the best.

Making Discoveries in the Dailies

What are you trying to find when you're first screening the material?

I look for stuff that's both visually beautiful and reveals something—sensitively shot, beautiful composition, interesting experiential stuff; material that I can make something out of. That will persuade people to feel that moment, the *life* of that moment.

What is the first thing you look for today, when determining how to approach the structure of a verité film?

I think audience. I think, what do people *need* to really get hooked into this story? And then, what can I use to continually bait the audience about what they may find out. When I can, I like to keep it mysterious—and *use* the mystery of what will happen next.

Can you give me an example?

Plan B, a film I did recently was about a fellow, Martin Kace, who became a paraplegic at 49 years of age. It was a POV kind of approach to what it is like to be a paraplegic. The shooting was very good, and the struggles were shot with a very experiential, subjective feel—verité at its best with a digital camera. I thought he was interesting enough as a person, that he had a lot of push in him, real determination—and he was going to do something that was pretty interesting: He was going to hang himself by his ankles with six or nine other paraplegics in the same position—in front of the Senate building. A photo op.

He planned to hang himself upside down as a political action? Can you describe the motivation behind this demonstration?

He wanted to create an icon that would leave an impression. He wanted to cause a stir in the press, and in Congress. Initially, the idea was it would represent how he felt society regarded him as meat, and then they said it represented life hanging in the balance. He was so bitter at that point. Of course that was the wrong concept, audiences would just be turned off. It was too bitter, and a bit wacko, really. He really pushed forward on it, though, and succeeded in doing it—hanging right side up with safety harnesses. But, in the end, it was a failure [in terms of attracting publicity; no members of the press showed up].

But you used this unusual publicity stunt as a narrative device to set up the desire and conflict in the film? Meaning, his desire was to call attention to the plight of paraplegics, and the need for stem cell research, and the conflict was achieving press attention?

I found that all to be a very interesting as a story line, and used the event as an engine to keep audiences wondering, "Is it going to happen?" and, "How is he going to do this?" And meanwhile, you're getting a sense of what life is like as a paraplegic. Such as, how does it affect the woman that you're living with?

Incidentally, I found her terribly charming, a wonderful woman. So she gave warm background elements to the story. It has everything I could work with, and I think it all worked pretty well.

What do you mean by that? What does it have?

Well, for one thing, it has an unknown character, which I like.

Why?

Well, he's an unknown character that you might want to know more about. He's a man of normal charm; he's not excessively charming like Marjoe or Arnold. But Kace has push, he has energy. [Kace was a semi-famous businessman, Russell Simmons's partner in his Phat Farm clothing company.] He has an interesting way of looking at himself, sometimes with humor. And he has a wonderful daughter who he talks to a lot, and this beautiful woman he's living with—to deepen the story line, to give it warm background feelings.

> *"He was going to hang himself by his ankles with six or nine other paraplegics."*

Describe the opening sequence, and how you eventually combined this material dramatically.

I used a totally superfluous scene to start the film, which I thought was wonderful. You see him driving into this little town in upstate New York, Columbia County, and he's musing about wanting to make a documentary film. So that introduces him as somebody who wants to make films. I like that. He wanted to make a documentary film about something that has nothing to do with what this film is, but you learn he's a guy who wants to do something meaningful. Then you hear the woman in his life describing how peripatetic he is, how much energy he has, and how nothing daunts him—tremendous energy and self-confidence. You don't know that he's a guy in a wheelchair at that point. He's just driving his van.

"Just like an artichoke— it keeps opening up."

But then she says, "He was this way..." So you begin to wonder. And *then* you realize he's in a wheelchair, and he's talking to this young guy, [another paraplegic] who's very charismatic, about what it would be like if they ever got their feelings back in their legs. And that draws you in. The guy says, "I want to pee on a rug. Stand up on my own two bare feet on a rug, and just stand there and take a piss." That got me—I thought that was the best way to hook them.

What happens after you've hooked the audience?

You've got all these different elements that are disparate, but it pulls you in, and gets you used to an interesting rhythm and pacing. It makes you want to stay with it. So then, he goes into rehab, and you see him crossing the street, heavy traffic on Sixth Avenue in the middle of a sunny day, and it's deafening noise, and he goes past this big diesel truck, and these guys are dynamiting in the streets on Sixth Avenue, and he's just rolling past them, breathing hard, and going up the sidewalk. In rehab he talks about, "Will I ever be able to cross my legs again?" So you feel sympathy for him. Then, he's telling the class what he wants to do—hang himself by his ankles in front of the Senate building.

To me that was a very, very effective way *into* the story. You see the class reacting to his demonstration plans, and he says, "I see you're sort of gulping and looking, like, what is he, crazy or something? I see you being astonished at what I want to do. How do people feel about that?" He's teaching a psychology class, so it's all very appropriate, what their reaction is. Because some of these students are going to be working in advertising, and he's trying to create an icon, so it's very relevant.

What were the students' reactions to his plan?

Of course, they're very negative. Their reactions are somewhat negative, and one of them is possibly supportive. But it just draws you in further, keeps getting you in further. Just like an artichoke—it keeps opening up. But you don't know what you're going to get in each leaf, what it reveals when you're opening it up.

Approaching the Edit

Put the audience first. Cut to enrich their viewing experience.

"As editors, we're thinking audience all the time. I've always said editors are proxy for audience. We love our audience, and we want them to be happy and be enriched. And we want them to stay with it, of course, especially if it's for television."

When screening dailies, be sensitive to the way the footage was captured. Try to see what the cameraperson saw in it, the life and meaning of the moment. But don't use material purely for its strong aesthetic values.

"Cameramen like what I do with their material, for obvious reasons. I respect the quality of what they're doing. I don't muscle it into some intellectual thing. I respect their curiosity. I *use* their curiosity. It matches my own. And of course, that doesn't mean that therefore I use only their best stuff. But, I'm certainly very sensitive to what I think is effective material. Very often I lose their best stuff, because it doesn't work."

Don't spoon-feed the audience. Trust them to discover the meaning of the film.

"To a lot of television producers, a documentary is like a term paper. They're not loving the audience, particularly. They believe you have to tell them what they're going to see, tell them what they're seeing, and tell them what they saw. There's an excessive use of narration in television because that's the one thing they know how to do, they were taught well in college and they know how to write. And the audience is just switching channels, or dozing off, because they're spoon-fed. So you have to wrestle with that, and argue for the audience. I would rather confront someone I'm working with than make a heavily scripted film that is totally boring the hell out of an audience."

You motivate the audience to keep watching by controlling the information they learn about the characters along the way.

Yes. And removing redundancies—the things that are diversions from the direction the film is going—to keep it moving it along.

It's like dropping breadcrumbs, almost, teasing them with unusual scenes of your main character's actions that pull them along by using curiosity.

When you're making documentaries, you don't have rape, you don't have murder, you don't have real mystery—you hardly have any humor. Certainly you don't have comedy—unless, it's about comedians or something. You don't have any of these great elements that feature editors have. So you've got to work with what you can work with that really *excites* you. And that's the secret of editing documentaries. You've got to find some way *into it*, unless it's a film that's totally academic.

Courage to Change Courses

You said earlier that an editor doesn't necessarily have to have an affinity for the subject of the film he or she is working on—that it sometimes helps to not know anything about the subject.

As long as he's curious, and loves footage, loves film, loves something with an interesting point of view that he can study and understand. That seems to be the rule. Now, when I edited a film on Willem de Kooning, I didn't like de Kooning. I had a prejudice against Abstract Expressionism from my old leftist days. The leftists were very negative about the American domination of Abstract Expressionism—that was part of our Imperialism drive, to dominate the world of art. That was my background, but I wasn't into dogmatism or anything. I'm always curious. So I loved de Kooning after working on the film.

Why?

I loved him as a person, I loved what he was trying to do, I liked the way he talked about it.

It's important to remain open to ideas that conflict with your own, while you're editing.

Yes, I'm very open. Very open in terms of the opinions I bring to the subject. I don't work on "cause" films, generally. I don't like to. If I believe in those causes it's

Appendix

Where to Buy Documentary Films

DOCURAMA
126 Fifth Ave 15th Floor
New York, NY 10011
Product information and availability: info@newvideo.com
Customer Support for products:
    customersupport@newvideo.com
Customer Support for online and phone orders:
    newvideo@ordering.com
Wholesale Sales, Acquisitions, and Marketing:
    docurama@newvideo.com
Retail Sales and Customer Support: (800) 314-8822
Wholesale Sales, Acquisitions and Marketing: (212) 206-8600
www.docurama.com

THIRD WORLD NEWSREEL
545 Eighth Avenue, 10th Floor
New York, NY 10018
(212) 947-9277
twn@twn.org
www.twn.org

WOMEN MAKE MOVIES
462 Broadway Suite 500WS
New York, NY 10013
(212) 925-0606
info@wmm.com (for general information)
orders@wmm.com (for film and videotape orders)
www.wmm.com

Notable Film Festivals that Feature Documentary Films

HUMAN RIGHTS WATCH
New York, New York
London, England
www.hrw.org/iff

FULL FRAME DOCUMENTARY FESTIVAL
Durham, North Carolina
www.fullframefest.org

SOUTH BY SOUTHWEST
Austin, Texas
www.sxsw.com

THE SUNDANCE FILM FESTIVAL
Park City, Utah
www.sundance.org

TRIBECA FILM FESTIVAL
New York, New York
www.tribecafilmfestival.org

Documentary Film Markets

HOTDOCS
Toronto, Ontario
www.hotdocs.ca

IFP MARKET
New York, New York
www.ifp.org

INTERNATIONAL DOCUMENTARY FILM FESTIVAL AMSTERDAM
Amsterdam, The Netherlands
www.idfa.nl/idfa_en.asp

MIPDOC
Cannes, France
www.mipdoc.com

Mastering Your Craft

DMTS™
Digital Media Training Series
http://www.digitalmediatraining.com/index.html

ZOOM IN™
The Quarterly DVD-based Guide for Digital Production
http://www.zoom-in.com

Professional Associations

ASSOCIATION OF INDEPENDENT VIDEO AND FILM
MAKERS
304 Hudson Street, 6th floor
New York, NY 10013
(212) 807-1400
info@aivf.org
www.aivf.org

INDEPENDENT FEATURE PROJECT (IFP)
Chapters in Chicago, Los Angeles, Miami, Minneapolis/
   St. Paul, New York, and Seattle
www.ifp.org

INTERNATIONAL DOCUMENTARY ASSOCIATION
1201 West 5th Street, Suite M320
Los Angeles, CA 90017 USA
(213) 534-3600
info@documentary.org
www.documentary.org

NEW YORK WOMEN IN FILM AND TELEVISION
6 East 39th Street, Suite 1200
New York , NY 10016
(212) 679-0870
info@nywift.org
www.nywift.org

Additional Information for Selected Films

After Innocence
Showtime
(2l2) 708–1582
http://www.afterinnocence.com/

American Dream
Miramax Home Video
(212) 625-5000
http://www.miramax.com/

Asylum
Filmmakers Library
(212) 808-4980
info@filmakers.com

Baseball
PBS Home Video
www.pbs.org
http://www.shoppbs.org/home/index.jsp

Bintou in Paris
Big Mouth Productions
(646) 230-6228
info@bigmouthproductions.com

Brooklyn Bridge
PBS Home Video
www.pbs.org
http://www.shoppbs.org/home/index.jsp

Brother Born Again
New Day Films
(888) 367-9154
http://www.newday.com/

Christo's Islands, Christo's Running Fence, and *Christo's*
   Valley Curtain
Plexi Films
(718) 643-7300
www.plexifilm.com

The Civil War
PBS Home Video
www.pbs.org
http://www.shoppbs.org/home/index.jsp

Daybreak Express
Pennebaker Hegedus Films
(212) 496-9195
www.phfilms.com

Deadline
Big Mouth Productions
(646) 230-6228
info@bigmouthproductions.com

Decade Under the Influence
New Video Group
(800) 314-8822
http://b2b.newvideo.com/

Derrida
Zeitgeist Films
(800) 509-0448
www.derridathemovie.com

Dinner for Five
Wellspring Media, Inc.
movies@wellspring.com
http://www.wellspring.com/movies/

The Donner Party
PBS Home Video
www.pbs.org
http://www.shoppbs.org/home/index.jsp

Dont Look Back
New Video Group
(800) 314-8822
http://b2b.newvideo.com/

Empire of the Air
PBS Home Video
www.pbs.org
http://www.shoppbs.org/home/index.jsp

Fahrenheit 9/11
Sony Pictures DVD & Video
(212) 833-6800
http://www.sonypictures.com/homevideo/index.html

Fast, Cheap, and Out of Control
www.errolmorris.com

Finding Christa
Hatch-Billops Collection
(212) 966-3231

The Flapper Story
The Cinema Guild
(212) 685-6242
http://www.cinemaguild.com/

Free Tibet
Ryko Distribution
(800) 808-RYKO

The Fog of War
www.errolmorris.com

Gimme Shelter
Criterion Films
mulvaney@criterionco.com
www.criterionco.com

Grey Gardens
Criterion Films
mulvaney@criterionco.com
www.criterionco.com

In Memoriam: New York City, 9/11/01
HBO
(212) 512-5000
http://www.hbo.com/

Innocent Until Proven Guilty
Big Mouth Productions
646.230.6228
info@bigmouthproductions.com

Jazz
PBS Home Video
www.pbs.org
http://www.shoppbs.org/home/index.jsp

Last Letters Home
HBO Home Video
(212) 512-5000
http://www.hbo.com/

Lewis and Clark
PBS Home Video
www.pbs.org
http://www.shoppbs.org/home/index.jsp

Marjoe
New Video Group
(800) 314-8822
http://b2b.newvideo.com/

Modulations
Iara Lee
reception@caipirinha.com
http://www.caipirinha.com/

Moon Over Broadway
New Video Group
(800) 314-8822
http://b2b.newvideo.com/

Monterey Pop
Criterion Films
mulvaney@criterionco.com
www.criterionco.com

The Paris Review: Early Chapters
Checkerboard Films
(212) 759-2056
www.checkerboardfilms.org

Primary
Drew Associates
(718) 238-7498
http://www.drewassociates.net/

Pumping Iron
Warner Home Video
(818) 954-6000
http://www2.warnerbros.com/web/video/index.jsp

Salesman
Criterion Films
mulvaney@criterionco.com
www.criterionco.com

Shelter Dogs
Cynthia Wade
http://www.shelterdogs.org/

Sit In (16mm only)
MacDonald & Associates
5660 North Jersey Avenue
Chicago, IL 60659

Startup.com
Pennebaker Hegedus Films
(212) 496-9195
www.phfilms.com

Sweet Toronto
Pennebaker Hegedus Films
(212) 496-9195
www.phfilms.com

The Thin Blue Line
www.errolmorris.com

Town Bloody Hall
Pennebaker Hegedus Films
(212) 496-9195
www.phfilms.com

Tupac: Resurrection
Paramount Home Video
(323) 956-5000
http://homevideo.paramount.com/index.jsp

Unzipped
Miramax
(212) 625-5000
http://www.miramax.com/

The War Room
Pennebaker Hegedus Films
(212) 496-9195
www.phfilms.com

Yanki No!
Drew Associates
(718) 238-7498
http://www.drewassociates.net/

Ziggy Stardust
Pennebaker Hegedus Films
(212) 496-9195
www.phfilms.com

Index

V

The Vagina Monologues, 284
Van Dyke, Willard, 302
van Slycke, Edith, 96
Vernon, Florida, 49, 50, 67
Village Voice, 80

W

Wade, Cynthia, 246
Wann, Jesse, 47–48
Ward, Geoffrey, 18
Warhol, Andy, 133
Warning Signs, 125
The War Room, 78, 80, 86, 104–105, 111, 343
Wasserman, Albert, 306
The West, 15
Wexler, Haskell, 88–89
Whalen, Richard, 97
White, Ryan, 116
White Paper, 305–306
Who's Afraid of Virginia Woolf?, 88
Wild Man Blues, 322, 327–331
Will, George, 30
Williams, Marco, 166–169
Williams, Ted, 27
Wiseman, Frederick, 21, 253
Women Make Movies, 340
Woodstock, 220
Working in Rural New England, 180
Wright, Frank Lloyd, 35

Y

Yanki No!, 217–218, 343
Yauch, Adam, 283–286
Young, Robert, 306

Z

Zapruder, Alexandra, 138
Ziggy Stardust, 100–101, 343
Ziskin, Laura, 72
Zoom In, 341